Nicolaus Copernicus

Making the Earth a Planet

Owen Gingerich
General Editor

Nicolaus Copernicus

Making the Earth a Planet

Owen Gingerich
and James MacLachlan

Oxford University Press
New York • Oxford

We fondly dedicate this book to our oldest grandchildren,
Philip Gingerich and Erin MacLachlan.

OXFORD
UNIVERSITY PRESS

Oxford University Press, Inc., publishes works that further
Oxford University's objective of excellence
in research, scholarship, and education.

Oxford   New York
Auckland   Cape Town   Dar es Salaam   Hong Kong   Karachi
Kuala Lumpur   Madrid   Melbourne   Mexico City   Nairobi
New Delhi   Shanghai   Taipei   Toronto

With offices in
Argentina   Austria   Brazil   Chile   Czech Republic   France   Greece
Guatemala   Hungary   Italy   Japan Poland   Portugal   Singapore
South Korea   Switzerland   Thailand   Turkey   Ukraine   Vietnam

Published by Oxford University Press, Inc.
198 Madison Avenue, New York, New York 10016
www.oup.com

Design: Design Oasis
Layout: Greg Wozney
Picture research: Ted Szczepanski

Library of Congress Cataloging-in-Publication Data

Gingerich, Owen.
Nicolaus Copernicus : making the Earth a planet / Owen Gingerich and
James MacLachlan.
p. cm.—(Oxford portraits in science)
Includes bibliographical references and index.
ISBN 0-19-516173-4
1. Copernicus, Nicolaus, 1473-1543—Juvenile literature. 2.
Astronomers—Poland—Biography—Juvenile literature. I. MacLachlan,
James H. II. Title. III. Series.
QB36.C8G46   2004
520'.92—dc22   2004020959

Printing number: 9 8 7 6 5 4 3 2 1

Printed in the United States of America
on acid-free paper

On the cover: *The 16th-century portrait in the background hangs in the town hall of Toruń,*
Poland. Both portraits were based on a now-lost self-portrait.
Frontispiece: *Copernicus holds a traditional armillary sphere, or model of the sky girdled by*
the zodiac, in this commemorative statue in Toruń, Poland, the city where he was born.

Contents

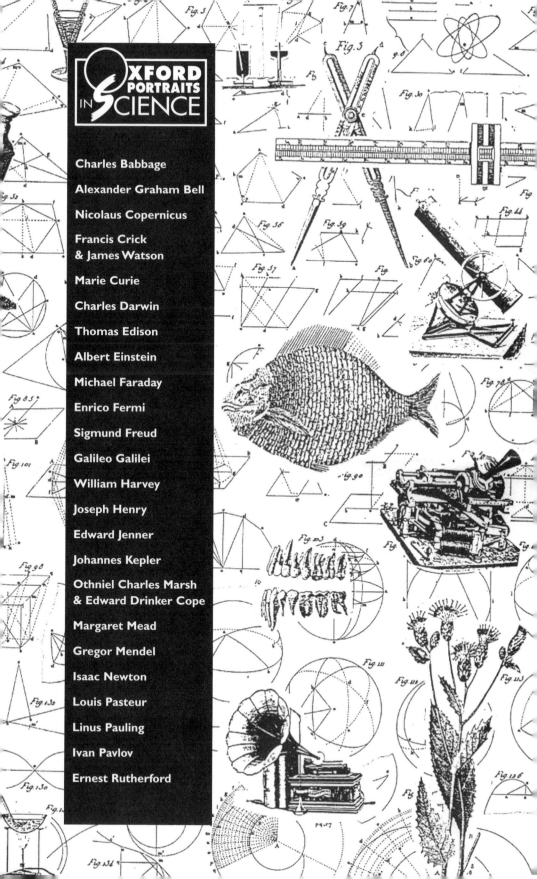

OXFORD PORTRAITS IN SCIENCE

CHAPTER

I

Expanding the World

The university hall was humming with conversations. At the beginning of the fall term in 1493, students at the Jagiellonian University in Cracow were renewing acquaintances after the summer break. Waiting for university officials to arrive, the students gradually gathered into buzzing clusters. Soon, one large group formed around a student from Vienna, standing on a chair waving a pamphlet.

The pamphlet contained a report from Christopher Columbus, a sea captain who had sailed westward across the Atlantic Ocean. He claimed that he had arrived at islands off the coast of Asia after sailing for 33 days from the Canary Islands near Africa. Could it possibly be true? He had brought back with him natives of those islands, who looked very different from Africans. He called them Indians. He also brought back gold and spices and forecast a rich trade with China for Spain. But the natives did not appear to be Asians. Was it possible that some new land blocked the westward route to the fabled East?

Andreas and Nicolaus Copernicus, from northern Poland, joined the students. They were returning for their third year at the university. More questions assaulted the

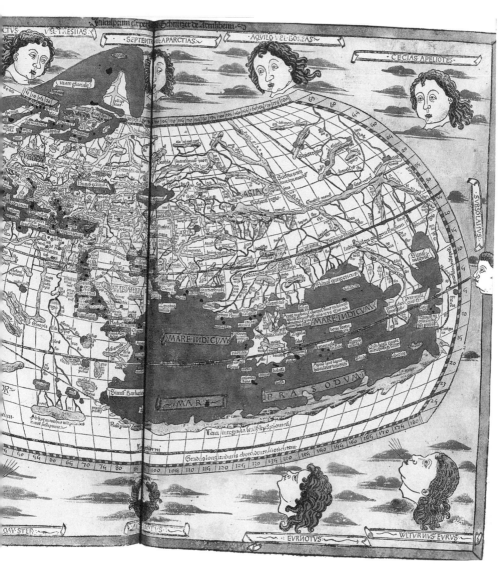

This world map, printed in Germany in 1482, reveals European knowledge of the world 10 years prior to Columbus's first voyage to the Americas. The mapmakers depicted the world using the positions of places tabulated by Claudius Ptolemy, the second-century astronomer and geographer.

student from Vienna. How far could Columbus have sailed in 33 days? About three thousand miles. Could Asia really be that close to Europe?

Another student reported that he had heard from Spain that Columbus had depended on scholars' estimates of the westward distance from Europe to Asia for his trip. One of the major sources had been a work written more than a thousand years before by the mathematician Ptolemy of Alexandria (in present-day Egypt). His *Geography* is an atlas giving the locations of cities all across the known world. Combined with reports from travelers to China, the locations Ptolemy provided indicated that a voyage to Asia would be only a few thousand miles—less than half the actual distance of more than 10,000 miles. Ancient geography turned out not to be as accurate as scholars had thought.

This small, gilded clockwork globe, a precious gift to the Jagiellonian University around 1510, is the earliest to show South America.

Nicolaus had already heard of Ptolemy in a different context. At about 150 CE, Ptolemy had created a work of astronomy that would hold sway in Europe for almost 1,400 years. His *Almagest* describes models for calculating the positions of stars and planets in the heavens at any time. Ptolemy based his mathematical models on the idea that the stars are on a great sphere centered on the earth and that the planets travel on various circular paths between the earth and the stars. Navigators found out where their ships were at sea by measuring the angles of stars above the horizon. Many people also believed that knowing the positions of the planets at specific times enabled astrologers to predict a person's fortune. This "casting of horoscopes" was a major reason medical doctors studied astronomy at university.

In succeeding years, Nicolaus and the other students would learn that the islands Columbus had explored were not off the coast of Asia. They belonged to the Americas, a great landmass that intervened between Europe and Asia. Soon, the outlines of the Americas began to appear on maps and globes in Europe. European powers were quick to send expeditions to plunder the wealth of these newly found lands. In the meantime, Nicolaus Copernicus devoted considerable spare time to revising Ptolemy's astronomy.

The 70 years of Copernicus's lifetime—from 1473 to 1543—marked great changes in Europeans' outlook on the world. In 1473 most people supposed that the searing heat from the sun at the equator would prevent sailors from ever crossing into the Southern Hemisphere. They believed that a great ocean surrounded Europe, Africa, and Asia, and that the only way to the spices of the Orient was by an overland route. A better understanding of the full extent of the world came in 1522 with the return of one ship of the Portuguese explorer Ferdinand Magellan's expedition completely around the globe. And Europeans in major cities learned of such voyages quickly, thanks to the printing industry that had begun only a few years before Copernicus's birth. The new printing presses made possible less expensive textbooks, illustrated encyclopedias, calendars, and prayer books. Nicolaus was a student in Italy from 1496 to 1503, at a time when arts and literature were in full flower during the Renaissance. The artists Raphael, Leonardo, and

The traditional earth-centered cosmos appears in this view of creation painted in the mid-15th century. In the center is the world, composed of the elements earth and water and surrounded by spheres of air and fire. The succeeding circles represent the transparent shells carrying the moon, Mercury, Venus, the sun, Mars, Jupiter, and Saturn. Above them all, God sets the shells into their swift daily rotations.

Michelangelo were painting and sculpting for wealthy patrons in Rome and Florence. Numerous scholars were translating Greek classics into Latin, to be spread across Europe as printed books.

Before Copernicus was 50, Martin Luther, a Catholic monk, began the revolt, known as the Reformation, against the authority of the Catholic Church. In 1517, he posted on the church door in the university town of Wittenberg, Germany, a list of 95 debating theses critical of church practices that had developed over the ages. Rapidly and widely distributed by printed copies, Luther's theses set off a revolt against the methods used by the church to raise money from even the poorest parishioners. Unscrupulous churchmen had encouraged people to pay money for a certificate (called an indulgence) to reduce the time they would spend in purgatory for their sins—people believed the more money they gave the greater the reduction in time. Many German princes, jealous of the money drained from their lands to Rome, joined in the protest, and eventually broke away from their traditional loyalty to the pope in Rome. They formed a new Protestant church. For the next hundred years, states and principalities fought wars over territories and religious authority. Only gradually did they achieve a new political and religious balance among Catholic and Protestant powers.

Copernicus worked in an exciting era of geographical

This highly imaginative view of Christopher Columbus discovering America was printed in Basel, Switzerland, in 1494, two years after his historic voyage. The addition of many oars to his sailing ship is one of several erroneous details.

exploration, religious reformation, and information explosion. He was born and died in Prussia, a province of Poland on the southern shore of the Baltic Sea. The word *Prussia* comes from the name of a Slavic people who occupied the southeastern shores of the Baltic around and between the mouths of the Vistula River, which flows northward to Gdańsk, and the Neman River to the east.

At the time of Copernicus, the kingdom of Poland occupied a dominant place in eastern Europe, but on its southern and eastern borders, Poland was under threat from the Muslim Ottoman Turks. To the north and along the Baltic coast, it was fighting off incursions from the German Teutonic Knights, who had for many years ruled the area and who still controlled the adjacent territories. Shortly before Copernicus was born, the Prussian lands came under the nominal rule of the king of Poland. However, the Teutonic Knights did not cede their power easily; through much of Copernicus's life, struggles between Poland and the Knights continued. Copernicus belonged to a diocese (territory controlled by a bishop) that owned lands the Teutonic Knights coveted. Although Copernicus was a churchman, he would eventually take charge of defending his territory against attacks by the Knights.

Copernicus lived in turbulent times, but he led a quiet life as a Catholic Church official in northeastern Poland, far from Renaissance centers, and he never participated in the fierce disputes between Catholics and Protestants. Yet, before his death he had initiated a renaissance and revolution of his own. He made the earth a planet orbiting the sun—challenging the two-thousand-year tradition of a motionless earth in the center of the universe. Although he was an obscure churchman in what he once called "this very remote corner of the earth," his revolution in astronomy would contribute greatly to transforming science in the centuries following his death.

CHAPTER 2

School Days in Poland

Nicolaus Copernicus, the youngest of four children, was born on February 19, 1473, in Toruń, a thriving town on the banks of the Vistula River in Poland. He was named after his father, a prosperous merchant, who had moved to Toruń from Cracow. In his early 40s, he married Barbara Watzenrode, who belonged to a prominent family of merchants in Toruń. "Nicholas" is the English spelling of the name Copernicus's parents gave their second son. It may have been originally "Niklas," and he may have been called "Nikkie" as a boy. However, when he left Toruń to go to school in Cracow, Niklas would become Nicolaus—the Latin spelling most commonly used at universities.

Toruń, where Nicolaus Copernicus grew up, lies about a hundred miles south of the Baltic Sea. In the 1470s it had about 10,000 inhabitants, including many merchants and mill owners engaged in foreign trade. They sent cloth, grain, and forest products by the Vistula River to the Baltic Sea, and from there to England, France, and other countries of western Europe. The bustling activities along the docks would have fascinated Nicolaus as a boy.

A. S. Johannis Kirch
B. S. Jacobs Kirch
C. S. Marten Kirch u. Gymn
D. Dominicaner Kloster
E. Kloster du m H. Geist
F. S. Laurenk Kirch

Toruń (or Thorn), the city of Copernicus's birth, with the Vistula River in the foreground, in a panorama from 1684. The 14th-century churches of St. John (A), St. James (B), and the Virgin Mary (C) still stand today.

The merchant's house (second from the left) where Nicolaus Copernicus was born, with its fancy double facades, is now a museum in the city of Toruń, Poland.

There were other places as well where young boys and girls could explore nature and history. An island in the middle of the Vistula River was heavily wooded and full of game. The river teemed with fish. Then there was the castle of the Teutonic Knights that the townsfolk had raided and destroyed only 20 years before Nicolaus was born. The ruins provided many caves and crevices in which young boys could play.

However, life was not all play. In school, Nicolaus had to learn to read and write, but not the German language he spoke at home. Rather it was Latin, the international language of Europe, the heritage of the Roman Empire from more than a thousand years earlier. So, besides spelling and grammar, he had to learn the meanings of a whole new set of words: *amo,* I love; *amas,* you love; *amat,* she/he/it loves; *amamus,* we love; and *puella,* the girl; *puellae,* of/to/for the girl; *puella,* by/with/from the girl. Memorize the lessons, play in the woods, go to church, and, at the end of a long day, take a candle up the narrow stairway to snuggle into a small wooden bed—that was his daily routine.

Nicolaus's father was active in the political affairs of those troubled times. Toruń lay in the southwest corner of the territory of Prussia, which is on the southeast coast of the Baltic Sea. Until the 1200s, Prussia had been the domain of pagan Slavic tribes. Christian rulers of eastern Europe invited warriors from the Crusades (a series of wars European Christians fought to rescue Jerusalem from the Muslims) to subdue the Prussians. The warriors belonged to the Order of Teutonic Knights. They conquered Prussia by building fortress towns at strategic locations, and then converted the Prussians to Christianity. The Knights continued to control Prussia for the next two hundred years.

For a while, Polish authorities in the south accepted the Teutonic Knights' Christianizing conquests in the province of Prussia. However, in the early 1400s, stronger rulers made Poland more unified, and they came to resent the Knights' control over their access to the Baltic. Moreover, merchants in the Prussian towns objected to having no part in Prussia's government. After some military successes, the Poles wrested control of western parts of Prussia from the Knights and gained access to the Baltic through Toruń to Gdansk at the mouth of the Vistula River.

For 40 years an uneasy peace reigned between Poland and Prussia. Conflict broke out again in 1454, during which time the senior Copernicus joined with other merchants of Toruń to lend financial support to the Polish king. Finally, in 1466, Poland was again victorious. In the peace treaty signed at Toruń in 1466, the knight-commander of the Teutonic

The astronomer's father kneels in prayer in this 17th-century copy of an older painting. The existence of such a pious portrait confirms that Copernicus came from a prosperous Catholic family.

At the Battle of Grunwalda, the Polish-Lithuanian army, led by King Wladyslav II Jagiello of Poland, defeated the knights of the Teutonic Order in 1410. It was one of the most horrendous battles Europe had known up to that time, with more than 40,000 soldiers killed in a single day.

Knights accepted the authority of the king of Poland and took the title Duke of Prussia. As young Nicolaus played around the ruins of the Teutonic Knights' castle in Toruń a few years later, he could not have known that he himself would have to do battle against these Knights in the coming years.

The climate of Toruń is much like that of Chicago or Toronto, except that summer highs are rarely above 25° C, or winter lows below -10° C. The Vistula River may be frozen for about three months in the winter. Although rain and snowfall are not excessive, humidity is generally high and the sky is often overcast. Yet Toruń is more than seven hundred miles closer to the North Pole than Chicago. It is as far north as Edmonton, Canada. As a result, young Nicolaus saw the sun set before 4 P.M. during December. At noon the sun hung low in the southern sky, only about 15° above the horizon. With less than eight hours of daylight at that time of year, Nicolaus got up and went to bed in the dark.

On clear nights in the winter, Nicolaus could gaze at thousands of stars twinkling like tiny diamonds in a black velvet sky. In our world of city lights and atmospheric pollution, it is rare to appreciate such a sight today. For night watchers five hundred years ago, a clear sky sparkled with points that outlined the figures of fabulous creatures:

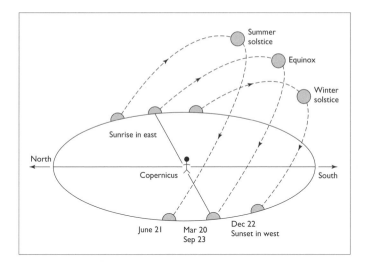

The dotted lines represent the path of the sun across the sky as seen from the latitudes of northern Poland at various key times of the year, the summer and winter solstices and the equinox.

Orion, the Great Bear, and dozens of other constellations. Watching for a couple of hours, Nicolaus could see that the constellations remained as permanent patterns but wheeled across the sky at the same rate (almost) as the sun in the daytime. For example, in the course of six hours, the Big Dipper traveled through an angle of 90°.

The whole starry system seemed to rotate about an imaginary line joining the earth's center to the North Star once a day. As the North Star remained nearly fixed about 53° above Nicolaus's northern horizon, why did the sun change its angle of elevation day by day? By the end of June, Nicolaus would see the noon sun at 60° above the horizon. Eventually he learned that the sun traces a path against the background of the stars in a plane that is tilted at 23.5° from the equator of the earth (and the starry sphere).

Nicolaus might have heard that northern peoples in ancient times held midwinter festivals to coax the sun to come back higher in the sky to restore the warmth of summer. Two thousand years before his time, Greek astronomers had shown the sun, stars, and planets, wheeling around on regular paths. And many people were convinced that the movement of the planets had influence on the course of

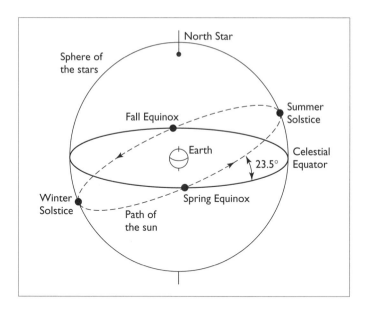

In the geocentric view that Copernicus studied as a schoolboy, the earth was fixed in the center of the cosmos. The sphere of stars spun around the earth each day, but as it spun the sun slowly moved along its tilted path, completing its circuit in a year.

human events. Although the church discouraged such astrological beliefs, they were widely held and provided a major reason for the study of astronomy. There is no evidence to suggest that astrology was a factor in Copernicus's interest in astronomy.

Sadly, when Nicolaus was 10, his father died. His two sisters were old enough to get on with their lives—his elder sister became a nun and his younger sister married a merchant—but the father's death made it less certain that the boys would be able to afford to attend university. Fortunately, their mother's brother came to the aid of the family. Lucas Watzenrode, age 36, was a member of the board of managers in two Catholic dioceses. Called canons of the cathedral chapter, these managers conducted the business affairs of each diocese, and were particularly in charge of collecting rents from the tenants of their considerable land holdings. While they accepted minor religious responsibilities, the canons were not necessarily ordained as priests.

Lucas was an ambitious man, eager to rise in the church hierarchy, and he extended his ambition to his young nephew

Nicolaus. He supported the Copernicus family while the boys completed their schooling. Nicolaus, besides improving his proficiency in reading and writing Latin, learned the basics of arithmetic and developed some skill in drawing. He had no inkling that these skills would eventually be put to use in advancing his interest in astronomy.

At 42, Lucas Watzenrode achieved his ambition of being elected bishop of Varmia with the concurrence of both King Casimir IV of Poland and Pope Innocent VIII. Varmia was a

A schoolmaster lectures to his pupils in this 16th-century woodcut. This school was for boys only, which was typical in Copernicus's day.

tract of two thousand square miles to the northeast of Toruń, almost entirely surrounded by the part of Prussia that was still ruled by the Teutonic Knights. The cathedral church of Varmia was located in Frombork on the Baltic coast, but the bishop's palace was situated in Lidzbark, 40 miles southeast of Frombork. As bishop of Varmia, Lucas was in effect the governor of the territory. As the chief administrator, he had considerable power over church appointments and could thereby enhance his family's fortunes; perhaps bright young nephew Nicolaus could follow in his uncle's footsteps.

The first order of business was to complete Nicolaus's schooling in Toruń. After that, in the autumn of 1491, Lucas enrolled Nicolaus and his older brother Andreas in Jagiellonian University in Cracow, where Lucas had himself been a student 25 years earlier. Nicolaus was now firmly set upon the road of his uncle's ambition. With hard work and influence in the right places, he, too, could become a bishop.

CRACOVIA

The Wawel Castle of the Jagiellonian kings stands high above the walled university town of Cracow, while the Vistula River flows around its battlements, in this woodcut from the Nuremberg Chronicle. The chronicle, the story of humanity up to the time of the book's publication in 1493, includes histories of several European cities.

At the University in Cracow

The Vistula River is navigable for another four hundred miles south of Toruń. Three or four days on a barge brought Nicolaus within sight of the royal city of Cracow, with the spire of the cathedral on the hill looming skyward before him. Beside it was a massive Gothic castle, the residence of King Casimir IV. Casimir's father, Wladyslav II Jagiello, founder of the Jagiellonian dynasty, had given his name to the university in Cracow almost a hundred years earlier.

Cracow was several times larger than Toruń, with a market square the size of four football fields. On all sides Nicolaus could feel the power and wealth of Poland. This was the Poland that his father and uncles had fought for a few years earlier. And now he was here to continue a glorious tradition. While Poland's strong Jagiellonian kings kept their enemies at bay, they also fostered studies in the arts and sciences to rival the older cultures of France and Italy. In particular, the university in Cracow had scarcely any rival in all northern Europe in the study of astronomy, for it had not just one, but two professors of astronomy.

A number of universities had begun in the early 1200s to prepare young men to be priests, doctors, or lawyers.

Women were not admitted until almost 1900. By the late 1400s scores of universities existed across Europe in many of the major cities. The program of studies was similar in all of them. Starting in their late teens, students enrolled first in the faculty of arts for four years. Some of them would then go on to more years in one of the faculties of theology, medicine, or law. Many who did not continue to those postgraduate studies became teachers.

Nicolaus Copernicus thus began his studies in the arts program at Cracow. Out of a total of 350 students in his class, about 150 were foreign, mostly from the German provinces to the south and west of Poland. With a total student body of about 1,500, the Jagiellonian University was more like one of today's liberal arts colleges than our great state universities with their many thousands of students. The language of instruction was Latin, and many of the lectures consisted

This courtyard of the Collegium Maius is the oldest part of Cracow University. Copernicus attended classes there from 1491 to 1495.

of reading and commenting on the texts of the Greek philosopher Aristotle. This curriculum continued with little change for another 150 years.

"Nicolaus, son of Nicolas," the eighth entry on this page of university records, shows that Nicolaus Copernicus has registered for the 1491–92 winter term at the University of Cracow and has paid his fees in full ("solvit totum").

More than 1,800 years before the time of Copernicus, Aristotle had conducted a school in Athens. For his students, Aristotle compiled and arranged the previous two hundred years of Greek scholarship, as well as adding a prodigious amount of text derived from his own studies. His numerous writings comprised a virtual encyclopedia of everything that was known at the time. And he put it all together into a tight system of logical relations, where everything depended on everything else.

Aristotle took the whole universe for his field of study. Typically his approach to any subject was to divide it into three categories. So, he divided his study of the universe into nature, God, and man. In nature he produced studies of the heavens, the earth, the classification of animal species, and meteorological features such as clouds, lightning, and meteors. All natural objects and the earth, he wrote, are composed of four elements: earth, water, air, and fire. The first two are heavy and have a natural tendency to move downward. The other two are light, and move naturally upward. From the sphere of the moon upward, the heavens are perfect and unchanging. They could not be composed of the four elements, so Aristotle proposed that the sun, stars, and planets consisted of a fifth substance, the ether. All ethereal objects moved naturally in circular motions.

For Aristotle, God was entirely a spirit, an all-knowing knower and an unmoved mover. It was God who kept the whole universe in order and in motion. Humans consisted partly of matter and partly of spirit. To account for the various parts of nature, Aristotle said that plants contained the soul of growth. To that was added a soul of motion for animals. And for humans he added a reasoning soul. God, on the other hand, was pure reasoning soul.

Notions such as these formed the basis for Copernicus's studies in Cracow. But how was it that the works of an ancient Greek philosopher had survived for so long? For a thousand years after the time of Aristotle, his manuscripts were copied and studied in a few academic centers in the lands around the eastern end of the Mediterranean. After 800 CE, Arab culture took up Aristotle's works as it flowered under Islam, the religion of Mohammed. Baghdad (in present-day Iraq), where Aristotle's works were translated into Arabic, was a particular focal point of scholarship. And when Islam spread across North Africa and into Spain, scholars took Aristotle's works with them.

In Spain after about 1000 CE, Islamic culture came into contact with the Latin culture of Europe. Europe had been in decline since the fall of the Roman Empire five hundred years earlier. Now Europeans found an advanced system of knowledge in Islamic culture in Spain. For the next two hundred years many of Aristotle's works were translated from Arabic into Latin. At the same time, several influential European scholars translated his writings directly from Greek into Latin. These Latin translations of Aristotle's works formed the foundation for the new universities that soon began to appear.

As European universities developed, their professors analyzed and commented on Aristotle's writings. Sometimes Copernicus studied books of commentaries, although he and his fellow students read Aristotle, too. Students also learned about mathematics and astronomy.

They studied the geometry of Euclid, a Greek who lived in Alexandria (in present-day Egypt) around 300 BCE. Euclid's textbook was still being taught in the early 1900s.

Copernicus's study of geometry trained him in logical relationships and gave him skills to study astronomy. The ancient Greek astronomer Claudius Ptolemy, who lived around 150 CE, had devised geometrical models to compute the positions of planets for any time in the past or future. In Baghdad, scholars translated his works (including those on astrology and geography) into Arabic. His work on astronomy, the *Almagest* ("the greatest" in Arabic), was translated into Latin at about the same time as Aristotle's works.

However, as the *Almagest* is very technical, the university professors normally taught a simplified version of basic astronomy. They very frequently used a small work written in the early 1200s by an English mathematician, John of Holywood.

In this scene of Aristotle teaching astronomers as imagined by a 13th-century Persian artist, the Greek philosopher is holding an astrolabe. This device was common in the 13th-century Arab world but unknown in the fourth century BCE when Aristotle lived. Although this astronomy class never happened, Aristotle did influence Arabs' understanding of astronomy through his writing.

text continues on page 31

Although some modern astronomy textbooks have sold in hundreds of thousands of copies, the astronomy textbook that has the greatest number of different printed editions was written almost eight hundred years ago. An Englishman, John of Holywood, who worked in Paris using the Latin form of his name, Johannes Sacrobosco, composed this short and simple textbook on the celestial sphere around 1220. His *On the Sphere* circulated in a manuscript version for two and a half centuries until it was first printed in 1476.

While Sacrobosco's *On the Sphere* served as a popular basic textbook, it said almost nothing about the motions of the planets. So, in the next generation, sometime around the middle of the 13th century, a more advanced textbook joined the ranks, Campanus's *Theorica planetarum*. The Latin words may tempt you to translate this as *Theory of the Planets,* but actually the meaning of *theorica* is more like "model" or "device." The book explains, in simple mechanical terms, how Ptolemy's theory worked.

Observations of each of the planets showed that they usually moved eastward against the background of stars, but sometimes, every year or so and at different times, each one stopped and then moved westward for a few weeks. This phenomenon is called *retrograde motion.* Around 150 CE the Alexandrian astronomer Claudius Ptolemy proposed a geometric model to account for this backward motion. His model involved two circles, one riding on the other. The bigger main "carrying" circle that went around the earth was called the *deferent* (the root *fer,* is the same as in the word *ferry*). The smaller circle, which was carried around on the deferent, was called the *epicycle.* In turn, the epicycle carried the planet itself. The combined motion of the two circles made the planet appear to move backward in the sky whenever the planet swung around into the inside, closest to the earth.

Soon after a German printer, Johannes Gutenberg, invented printing by movable type in the 1450s, a professor of astronomy at the University of Vienna, Georg Peurbach, wrote an updated version of the *Theorica.* (By the way, Georg is the German spelling of George, and it is pronounced Gay-Org.) His *Theoricae novae planetarum* was a new textbook on Ptolemy's

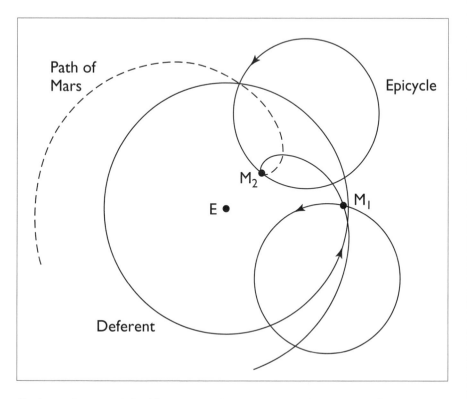

Path of Mars

Epicycle

M_2

E •

M_1

Deferent

The diagram shows to scale the deferent and epicycle that produces Mars's retrograde loop. The same epicycle is shown here in two positions as it carries Mars around from M_1 into its retrograde loop at M_2.

planetary models (*not* "new models"). However, Peurbach included an idea that had become popular during the Middle Ages. He tried to show how Ptolemy's deferents and epicycles could be embedded within a framework of transparent, crystal material, thereby building an actual picture of how the cosmos could be constructed.

Aristotle had proposed that the love of God spun the heavens every 24 hours. The system of crystal spheres gave an idea of how the motions could be transmitted mechanically from the outside in to the solidly fixed Earth in the center of the system. God in heaven, beyond the sphere of fixed stars,

continues on page 30

continued from page 29

could generate all the spin needed to keep the heavenly clockwork going. This structure fit perfectly with Christian, Jewish, and Islamic ideas about the nature of the created universe. It was against this deeply ingrained picture that Copernicus began to consider a radical alternative scheme.

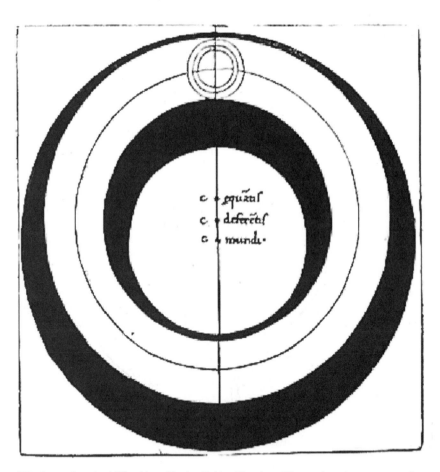

This diagram from the 1473 edition of Peurbach's New Theories of Planets *shows how structures of celestial crystal (the two thick, black rings) could be arranged to match observations of the planets. When rotated, the rings drive the planetary epicycle along the channel between them. This model could be applied to Mars, Jupiter, and Saturn.*

text continued from page 27

His text, *On the Sphere,* did little more than describe the shape of the heavens and the earth, and explain such things as the seasons. In Copernicus's very first year at Cracow in the winter of 1491, the university's astronomy course used this text, and he undoubtedly listened to these lectures.

In the winter of 1492, the university offered lectures on Euclidean geometry. By now the teenage Copernicus had begun his lifelong love affair with mathematical astronomy. He obtained a copy of Euclid's *Geometry,* which had been printed for the first time in 1482, and a Latin translation of an Arabic text on astrology.

Later, in the summer term of 1493, Copernicus learned about the motions of the planets from a recent update of a traditional book on planetary theory. Like every astronomy book then available, it assumed that the earth was fixed at the center of the universe, and the planets revolved around it. Georg Peurbach wrote *New Theories of the Planets* in Vienna in the 1450s. His book discussed the old planetary geometry, but it also included a new treatment of how the old models derived from Ptolemy could be fit together. Often reprinted, Peurbach's book initiated an enlarged interest in technical astronomy throughout Europe. Before his early death at age 38, he had begun an improved translation of Ptolemy's *Almagest.* His work was continued by his pupil Regiomontanus, whose publications became of great importance to Copernicus.

To be able to cast horoscopes, students needed more advanced courses to learn to use tables of planetary motion so that they could find the positions of the planets for the date of the horoscope. In the winter term of 1493, Copernicus heard lectures on the *Tabulae resolutae* (Handy tables), astronomical charts that were especially popular in Cracow. Perhaps it was at this time that he obtained and had bound together printed copies of two sets of astronomical tables, along with 16 blank pages for extra notes. One, the

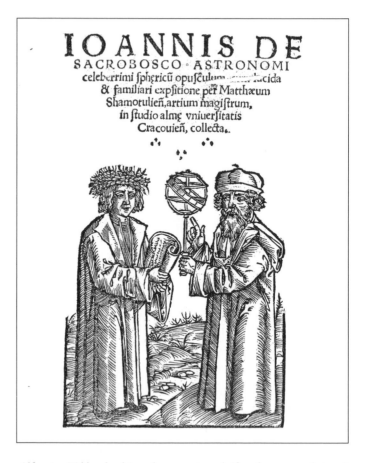

IOANNIS DE
SACROBOSCO · ASTRONOMI
celeberrimi fphæricū opufcŭlum ...... lucida
& familiari expfitione per Matthæum
Shamotulieñ,artium magiftrum,
in ftudio almę vniuerfitatis
Cracouieñ, colleca.

Alfonsine Tables, had just been printed (for the second time)
in Venice in 1492. The other, compiled by Regiomontanus
in 1467, was printed in Augsburg, in southern Germany, in
1490. On several of the blank pages Copernicus copied parts
of a table by Peurbach. They indicated times of eclipses of
the sun and moon, and a set of latitude tables. Evidently, the
star-struck youth was becoming immersed in astronomy.

Nicolaus left the university in 1495, after four years in
the faculty of arts, but without taking a degree. The degree
would only be needed for teaching, and Nicolaus expected
his uncle, Bishop Lucas Watzenrode, had other plans for
him. He set off for Frombork to find out what his uncle
would decide. If he undertook further studies, Nicolaus was
confident he could pass any required entrance examinations.

Historians know only a little about Nicolaus's brother Andreas. At every stage of life except birth and death he seems to have followed behind his younger brother. He died 25 years before Nicolaus, in 1518. Even when they enrolled at the university in Cracow, Uncle Lucas seems to have had less faith in Andreas's ability than in that of his younger brother. Records show that Nicolaus paid his full fee, but Andreas did not—perhaps he did not carry a full load of courses. Nicolaus enrolled for graduate study in 1496, while his brother enrolled two years later. In 1499, Andreas was called a "cleric of Chelmno," but Nicolaus had had that title three years earlier, with both appointments arranged by Uncle Lucas.

Shortly after Nicolaus arrived in Frombork in 1495, one of the 16 canons of the Cathedral Chapter of Varmia died. Uncle Lucas nominated Nicolaus to fill the vacancy. However, the rule at the time required final approval of appointments in an odd-numbered month by the Vatican. As the vacancy had to be filled in September (an odd-numbered month), Bishop Watzenrode did not have the final authority, and for several months the appointment was under dispute for reasons now unknown—perhaps there was a rival candidate. Eventually the matter was settled so that Nicolaus was securely in the position well before his older brother Andreas received his nomination in the summer of 1501.

Still, at age 24, Nicolaus was uncertain about the career he should follow. Then in the summer of 1496, Lucas arranged for Nicolaus to take the next step along the path he himself had followed. He sent Nicolaus to study church law at the University of Bologna in Italy. We do not know if Copernicus had appealed for a chance to continue astronomical studies. As he depended on his uncle for support, he had little say in the matter. But he did make sure to include his precious book of astronomical tables in his baggage.

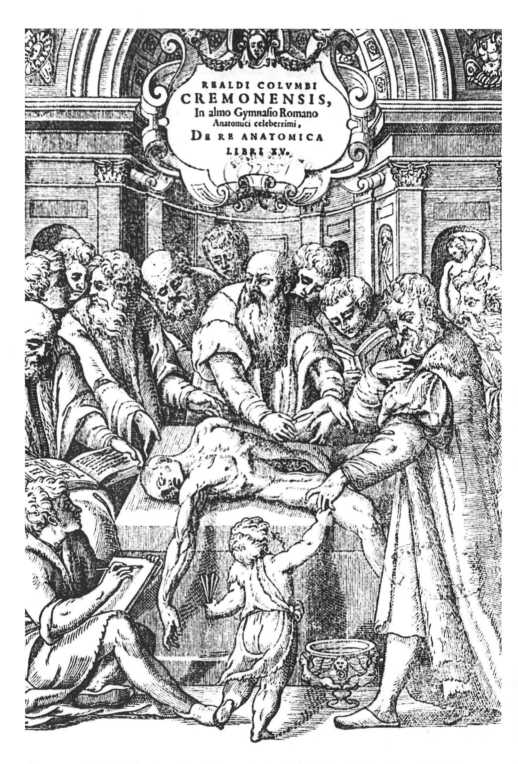

RBALDI COLVMBI
CREMONENSIS,
In almo Gymnafio Romano
Anatomici celeberrimi,
DB RB ANATOMICA
LIBRI XV.

A surgeon, usually a barber, dissects a corpse before a group of medical students while the professor (at the left) reads the instructions. The illustration is from the title page of an anatomy textbook published in Venice in 1559.

A Scholar
in Italy

In September 1496, Nicolaus Copernicus set out for Bologna. After visiting friends in Toruń and Cracow, he followed the busy five-hundred-mile packhorse route through Vienna to Venice. Seventy miles farther on lay the ancient city of Bologna, already important as a crossroads in Roman times. This walled city of a hundred towers amazed Nicolaus with its many covered sidewalks, so different from the more open construction of Polish cities.

Lectures at the University of Bologna began near the end of October. Nicolaus found the organization very different from that at Cracow. Students were placed in various "nations" according to their native language. Nicolaus enrolled in the German nation. At the head of each nation was a student, not a faculty member. The university, although founded before 1200, had no buildings of its own. It was composed of the professors the student nations chose to hire. The professors taught in their own homes. Bologna was the foremost university for legal instruction in all of Europe. Its total student population was two or three times larger than Cracow's.

Nicolaus was familiar with the form of instruction the university provided: the professor (or sometimes a senior

Like many 15th-century cities, the university town of Bologna, where Copernicus studied law, sat behind secure walls that protected it during times of war. This view was published in the 1493 Nuremberg Chronicle, which was one of the first books to successfully combine pictures and text, printing technology that would later be critical to the production of Copernicus's own book.

student) read from the text and made comments on it. The chief text in the faculty of law was the *Decretals* (the Latin word for "decisions"), an organized collection from about 1150, composed of decisions by popes regarding authority and behavior within the jurisdiction of the church.

The *Decretals* is arranged in five divisions: the authority of judges; the procedures and rules for making judgments; the rights and duties of the clergy—from priests to the pope—on holding property and conducting the Holy Sacraments; all the rules and regulations for marriage; and the penalties for various offenses. These decisions for governing the church are known as canon law. Canon law was different from civil law, which was administered by kings and other rulers as well as town councils. Some lawyers became certified in both types of law; Nicolaus studied both but concentrated on canon law.

Canon law was particularly important in that period because the pope in Rome exerted great authority across Europe in matters of state as well as of church. For example, priests who committed civil crimes (such as theft or murder) were subject only to canon law. Thus, church officials were above the civil laws. If Nicolaus was to become an effective church official back in Varmia, he would do well to pay close attention to his lessons.

As long as his uncle held the purse strings, Nicolaus had to be careful with his expenditures. Clothing, lodging, and entertainment were expensive in Bologna. When he heard the news that opposition to his becoming canon in the Varmia Cathedral Chapter had at last been overcome, Nicolaus fully expected to get the post. He was so confident that on September 20, 1497, he went to a local notary public (an official who could authenticate documents) to establish his claim. The notary drew a document that entitled two representatives in Varmia to act on his behalf in collecting his income:

> Nicolaus, son of the late Nicolaus Copernicus, being a canon of [V]armia and a student of canon law in Bologna is present here before me to authorize [two proxies in Varmia] to act in his name to receive, accept, and make decisions on any and all freeholds and estates, and whatever property, movable and immovable, rights, actions, income, and benefits are due to him from any canonries still vacant.

Now Copernicus would have an income that did not come directly from his uncle. But before he could begin to make his own financial decisions, he realized that he had been too hasty. He had not yet received official confirmation of his appointment. That arrived a couple of weeks later, and he returned the document to the notary to have the date changed. The notary crossed out "September 20" and wrote instead "October 10." Now, it was all legal.

However he felt about his future, Copernicus continued his studies in Bologna while on leave from his duties as a canon of Varmia. His brother Andreas (now also a canon) joined him for a brief time at the university, and in 1499 the two managed to convince a representative of the Varmian chapter to advance them a year's worth of income in order to be able to participate fully in Bologna's student life. By this time, Copernicus had already found an opportunity to reengage himself with astronomy.

Early in 1497, Copernicus took lodgings with Domenico Maria da Novara, the 43-year-old professor of astronomy at Bologna. He assisted Novara with his observations, and began to expand his own knowledge of astronomy. He obtained a copy of the *Epitome of the Almagest*, Regiomontanus's perceptive summary of Ptolemy's astronomy, which had just been printed in Venice in 1496. With that book in hand, Copernicus could delve much more deeply into the mathematical foundations used to derive astronomical tables. That required him to be able to

Regiomontanus's abridged version of Ptolemy's Almagest (1496) was the first printed book to include the technical details of the earth-centered, epicyclic astronomy. Both Ptolemy (left) and Regiomontanus (right) appear on the elaborate frontispiece of the book.

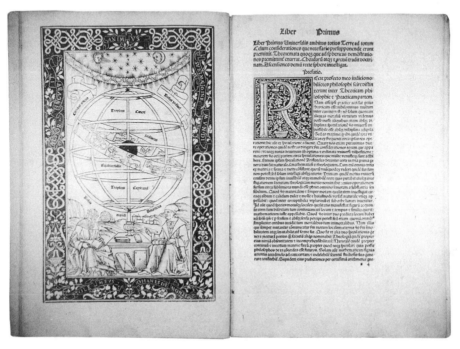

calculate lengths and angles in triangles (the branch of mathematics known as trigonometry).

Copernicus soon realized that Ptolemy's models for the orbits of the planets deviated considerably from the principles of perfection that Aristotle had laid down. This did not mean that Ptolemy was wrong: his models provided good predictions for the positions of planets at future times. But they did not follow the ideal of geometric perfection.

The early philosophers thought the heavens moved eternally in perfect circles because motion in a circle can continue forever without beginning or end. They also thought that the motion within the circle should be uniform, not speeding up or slowing down. And to complete the principles of perfection, the circles were centered on the earth itself.

These theoretical requirements were very difficult to achieve in practice, however. The orbit of the sun is a good example of the problem. People who have not thought about this problem might suppose that the four seasons have equal length, about 91¼ days each. However, even before the time of Ptolemy, Greek mathematicians had noted the unequal lengths of the seasons: spring, 92¾ days; summer, 93¾ days; autumn, 89¾ days; and winter, 89 days. This meant that either the sun is moving faster in its orbit in winter, making that season shorter, or else the circular orbit of the sun needed to be displaced from the earth so the sun moves through the winter quarter of the sky more quickly.

With his developing skills in trigonometry, Copernicus could follow the explanation Ptolemy had used. The sun could be seen as moving uniformly in an offset circular path, centered about a point whose distance from the center of the earth was about 3.5 percent of the distance from the earth to the sun.

It is tempting to imagine that according to Ptolemy, the sun zoomed around this offset orbit every day as it rose in

text continues on page 43

T he complicated observed motion of Mars provided a great challenge both to Copernicus and to his ancient predecessor, Ptolemy. The most conspicuous feature of Mars's motion occurs approximately every two years, when the planet becomes very bright, stops its normal eastward motion against the starry background, and for several weeks moves westward or in "retrograde."

The diagram shows the patterns of retrograde motion for Mars during 17 years in Copernicus's lifetime. The Polish astronomer observed Mars in 1504 and wrote a cryptic comment in one of his books noting that "Mars is ahead of the tables by 2 degrees, and Saturn is behind by 1½ degrees." Modern calculations compared with the almanacs of his day show this was true in 1504. Two of Copernicus's records of the positions of Mars from 1512 are preserved in his great book, *Revolutions*.

Mars goes into retrograde motion every 780 days—that is, slightly more than two years. Each time, the retrogression is approximately 55 degrees farther around the zodiac, the band of

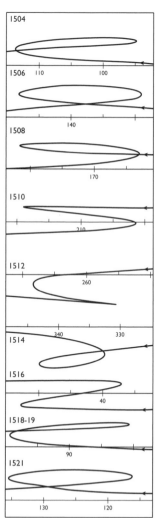

In this diagram of the retrogressions of Mars from 1504 to 1521, the horizontal lines represent small sections of the ecliptic circle— the exact path of the sun across the sky, which the planets follow approximately—where Mars's retrograde motion took place. The lines are divided into five-degree intervals. At the start of the sequence, in 1504, Mars retrograded through northern latitudes, so it is shown above the ecliptic. But in successive retrogressions the pattern moved southward, going below the ecliptic, and then back north again. This happened because the plane of Mars's orbit is tilted with respect to the earth's. Can you deduce the direction of the tilting? Notice that after about 15 years the pattern begins to repeat

the sky where the planets move. Mars's path was different each time. The longest retrogression, in 1506, was nearly twice as long as the shortest one, in 1514. The lengths and shapes came back to a similar pattern when the retrogressions had moved all the way around the sky, so that the pattern in 1518–19 was similar to the one in 1504.

If Ptolemy had used only a deferent centered on the earth and an epicycle, his geometrical device would have always produced retrogressions of the same size. Ptolemy searched for some additional device to make the predicted patterns for Mars match the ones he could observe. One way to do this was to move the deferent circle slightly off-center from the earth. This is called an *eccentric*. If the epicycle moves around the deferent at a uniform speed, from the earth it will look as if it is moving faster when the eccentric circle brings the epicycle closer to the earth. In fact, Ptolemy knew that Mars appeared to move fastest when it was passing through the constellation

continues on page 42

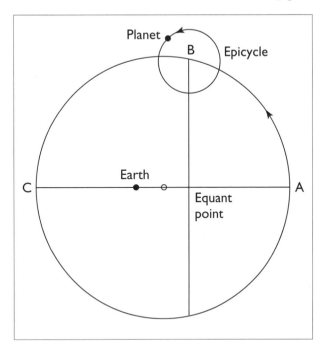

The epicycle center must move from A to B in the same time it takes to go from B to C, but because the deferent is farther from the equant at C than at A, there is farther for the epicycle to go, and therefore the epicycle with its planet moves faster near C and slower near A.

continued from page 41

Aquarius, and slowest on the opposite side of the sky. The eccentric worked just fine for making Mars go faster or slower. Unfortunately, it failed miserably in predicting the different sizes and shapes of the retrogressions.

At this stage Ptolemy was very ingenious. Instead of having the epicycle move on the deferent at a constant speed about its center, he chose a different point to center the constant angular speed, or rate of rotation. He located this *equant* point at the same distance from the center as the earth, but on the opposite side. To see how an equant works, look at the figure on page 41. The 360° around the equant have been divided into four equal 90° quadrants, so the angular motion in each quadrant is the same. The epicycle center must move from A to B in the same time it takes to go from B to C. But, because the deferent is farther away at C than at A, there is farther for the epicycle to go, and therefore it moves fastest near C and slowest near A. Ptolemy must have been very pleased with himself when he discovered that this simple arrangement closely approximated both the varying speed of the planet and the different lengths of the retrogressions.

Earlier Greek philosophers had taught that the unending celestial motions should be explained with circles and with constant speeds. Later astronomers were not always so satisfied with Ptolemy's solution, because the equant produced a non-constant speed on the epicycle. This, they believed, was cheating, or at least it was not philosophically pleasing. During the medieval period, Islamic astronomers working in Persia and Syria invented alternative schemes that used small circles called epicyclets to produce the same results without an equant device. It was one of these arrangements that Copernicus would incorporate into his own cosmological system.

text continued from page 39

the east, crossed the sky, set in the west, and continued around on the other side of the earth. Actually, the sun went around in its offset orbit only once a year, but the offset orbit itself whirled around the earth every day. The offset orbit was fixed with respect to the stars, and they, too, spun around every day with the offset orbit of the sun and the orbits of the other planets. Because, according to Aristotle, they were all made of weightless, celestial ether, this system seemed logical.

Compared to the planets, the sun's orbit was easy. Ptolemy found he could not represent the more complex motion of Mars, for example, simply by a circular orbit offset from the earth. It was much more complicated, and Ptolemy adopted a solution in which Mars moved at a nonuniform speed. This was a problem that Copernicus turned over and over in his mind. The observed motion of Mars was clearly not uniform. Sometimes Mars moved more slowly than average and sometimes more quickly. And about once every two years, Mars's eastward progress among the stars slowed, stopped, and reversed for several months before resuming its eastward direction. When a

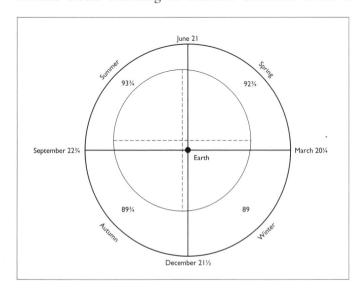

In Ptolemy's model, although the sun moved uniformly around its off-center circle (the inner circle in this diagram), from the earth the sun appeared to stay longer in the summer quadrant, 93 ¾ days, than in the winter quadrant, 89 days. The speed of the sun through the seasons was measured by the angular speed, that is, the rate of rotation, from the offset earth—not from the center of its orbit, the dashed axis in this diagram.

planet slowly moves west against the starry background, it is said to be in retrograde.

In order to account for this backward motion, Ptolemy showed the planet moving in a combination of two circles with continuous counter-clockwise motion. The planet moved in a small circle called the epicycle, which in turn moved in a large circle around the earth. The motions in the circles never stopped, and the combination made the planet, as seen from the earth, appear to stop and then move retrograde. It was very clever.

However, from time to time in the centuries after Ptolemy, scholars had doubts about Ptolemy's models. This was not because the models were not clever or that they failed to predict correct positions for the planets, but because they violated some of the ancient ideas about how eternal, celestial motions should be explained. In order to conform as much as possible to Aristotelian principles, Ptolemy had confined his models to various combinations of circular motions. But to make it work in detail, the motion of the smaller circle (epicycle) riding on the larger circle had to be nonuniform. Ptolemy apologized for this departure from good philosophical principles, but he knew something of the sort was required to explain the observations, and he chose a combination of two relatively simple ways to do it. He offset the larger circle from the earth, and he chose still another point (the equant) as the center of uniform motion. The equant complicated the model, but it was not very difficult to calculate its effect and could be worked into the calculation of planetary tables.

Arab astronomers of the Middle Ages found the equant procedure particularly disturbing. They would not consider motion on a circle uniform unless it was uniform about the actual center of the circle, not some other point offset from the circle's center. They proposed several ways to avoid using Ptolemy's equant, all of which required the use of one or more small auxiliary circles called epicyclets. Some European astronomers learned about these devices, and eventually Copernicus, too, found out about them, though he may never have known that these ideas came from Arab astronomers.

Copernicus saw that there was a job to be done: Ptolemy's models needed to be revised to conform to Aristotelian principles. On and off for the next half-dozen years, he worried over this problem. Eventually he would find an answer.

Copernicus extended his understanding of planetary models by working through the *Epitome* whenever he could during spare time from his legal studies. He was still responsible to the Cathedral Chapter in Frombork to prepare himself to take on his duties as canon when he returned to Varmia. In the summer of 1500 he had completed four years in the faculty of law at Bologna. Without taking examinations for a degree, Nicolaus and Andreas went as tourists to Rome for a few months.

This was a jubilee year in Rome, celebrating 1,500 years of Christianity. Pope Alexander VI spared no expense on opulent entertainment for the jubilee. He also spent great sums of money on buildings and decorations. Rome, along with other cities in the Italian peninsula, was reaching the high point of the literary and artistic transformations of the Renaissance. Scholars strove to write the elegant Latin they learned from ancient Roman writers such as Cicero and Virgil. Artists portrayed their subjects in scenes that resembled nature much more closely than had those of earlier centuries. The pope even consulted with the painter Michelangelo on the rebuilding of St. Peter's Basilica, a center for the Catholic Church in Rome.

Alexander VI's exorbitant spending of funds that were extracted from faithful Christians would soon lead to calls for reform of the church, especially in Germany, where a Catholic monk, Martin Luther, was leading the reform movement. The Germans were also not at all pleased by the wealth that this profligate pope squandered on his

text continues on page 48

THE MYTH OF EPICYCLES-ON-EPICYCLES

In the centuries immediately preceding Copernicus, the most common way to calculate the positions of planets was to use the *Alfonsine Tables.* These tables gave starting positions at specified dates for each of the planets, plus information about how far each planet moved per day. There were also extensive tables of corrections, because the speed of each planet as seen from Earth was far from uniform. Copernicus obtained a set printed in 1492 while he was a student at Cracow. These tables had been assembled in Paris around 1320, and were based on an earlier (but now lost) set of tables made by astronomers working under the patronage of King Alfonso X of Spain in the 1270s.

A very old legend says that when Alfonso watched his astronomers at work, he remarked that if he had been present at creation, he could have given the Lord some hints. This anecdote suggests that King Alfonso thought the motions of the planets were too complicated. Partly as a result of this story, a myth grew that Alfonso's astronomers had been obliged to use not just one epicycle for each planet, but a whole series of small epicycles on epicycles.

In reality, the entire arrangement of the *Alfonsine Tables* depended on the idea that each planet had only one independent epicycle. To have included another epicycle would have made the tables so complicated that no medieval mathematician could have coped with them. Nevertheless this story is so widespread in modern scientific culture that physicists and astronomers sometimes use the expression, "But perhaps my theory has too many epicycles," to apologize for an unduly complicated scientific explanation.

Historians of astronomy have nevertheless discovered that Islamic astronomers did experiment with adding one or more extra circles to Ptolemy's original proposal. They did this not to account for some small complication of planetary movement, but to make what they thought was a more pleasing theory. Because the heavenly motions were eternal, they believed that the paths of the planets should be explained with uniform movement in perfect circles. Ptolemy cheated, they believed, by using his equant. Although the motion around the equant point was on the circle, it was sometimes faster and sometimes slower.

How could the Islamic astronomers replace the equant with uniformly moving circles? In the 13th century, Nasir al-Din al-Tusi, working at the

Maragha Observatory (in present-day Iran), added two small circles that accomplished the same motion as the equant. Later, in Damascus, Ibn al-Shatir arranged the circles somewhat differently. Because these little circles were not independent in their motion but were locked into a particular angle depending on where they moved on the larger circle, the planetary tables did not become more complicated.

Like the Islamic astronomers, Copernicus was offended by Ptolemy's equant, and he believed his system would be more aesthetically appealing if he could eliminate it. Curiously enough, he initially proposed to use the same mechanism that Ibn al-Shatir had invented. Copernicus could not read Arabic (the language in which Ibn al-Shatir wrote), and no one has been able to explain how Copernicus could have found out about it. However, it seems likely that a 15th-century Viennese astronomer, Johannes Angelus, used such an arrangement to compute the planetary positions for his almanacs. Copernicus knew about these almanacs and remarked that Angelus had some special procedure, so perhaps the idea was "in the air" even though Copernicus had no clue about its actual origin.

Copernicus aimed to replicate the planetary motion described by Ptolemy's earth-centered equant model with his sun-centered epiclyclet model, which eliminated the equant. In his model Copernicus moved the center of his circle halfway between Ptolemy's equant and center. In order to keep the planets' motion on the same path as in the equant model, shown with the dashed circle on the right, Copernicus introduced an epicycle with a diameter equal to the distance between the center and the equant in Ptolemy's model. In the equant model the motion about the center is not uniform, but in Copernicus's model there are two uniform motions around separate centers—the center of the circle and the center of the epicycle.

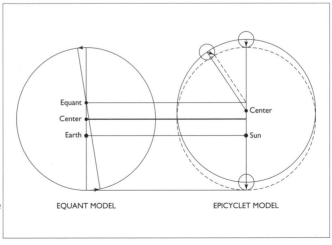

EQUANT MODEL   EPICYCLET MODEL

text continued from page 45

illegitimate children, nor with reports that as a wealthy cardinal he had simply bought the papacy.

Visiting Rome for the first time, Andreas and Nicolaus gaped in awe at the magnificent buildings and the lavish ceremonies. They remained in Rome for a few months. Four decades later Nicolaus Copernicus recalled for a young disciple, Georg Joachim Rheticus, that while in Rome he had lectured on mathematics to a large crowd of students, important men, and experts; unfortunately nothing more is known about the occasion or about his visit to Rome.

Near the end of July 1501, the two brothers appeared at a meeting of the Varmian Cathedral Chapter in Frombork.

The European cities important for Copernicus's life and works are labeled in bold type.

They asked to be allowed to return to Italy to study. The report of that meeting demon-strates the chapter's higher regard for the younger Nicolaus than for Andreas. The chapter readily granted Nicolaus a two-year extension because he "promised to study medicine with the intention of advising our most reverend bishop in the future, as well as members of our chapter, as a healing physician." Andreas, however, sought to begin his studies "according to the statutes." He apparently felt he needed to appeal to the rule that allowed a canon to be absent for studies, even though the statute required him to "devote his energies solely to his studies without interruption for three full years." The chapter's permission sounds grudging: "Andreas also seemed qualified to engage in studies." It is not known if he ever completed those studies, but, in 1502, he represented Varmia in Rome in a dispute with the Teutonic Knights.

Copernicus drafted this document for a notary in Padua, where he was studying medicine, in order to receive the income from a church in Wroclaw, a city northwest of Cracow. Written on January 10, 1503, this is his earliest dated signature.

In October 1501, Nicolaus enrolled as a medical student at the University of Padua, the leading faculty for medicine in all of Europe. As in arts and law, lectures consisted of readings from ancient Greek texts, translated into Arabic, and then into Latin. Medical practice in the 16th century was still largely based on the teachings of Galen, a second-century Roman from Asia Minor with a reputation as the most prolific, cantankerous, and influential of ancient medical writers. Galen was still a chief authority for medical practice, even though his writings dated back more than a thousand years. When there were medical dissections, the professor at the podium read from Galen's text.

When Copernicus was studying medicine in Padua, the "blood-letting man" was a standard feature of medical astrology. According to medical knowledge of the time, doctors trained in astrology could determine where on the body to "bleed" a patient depending on which sign of the zodiac was about to rise in the east.

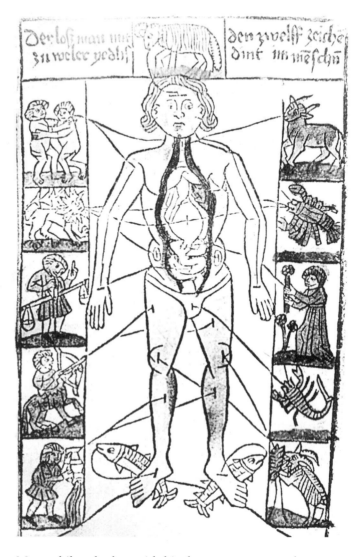

Meanwhile, a barber with his sharp razor cut up the corpse according to what the professor read. It is unlikely that students saw what Galen said they should.

Galen believed that good health depended on the balance of four bodily fluids: blood, phlegm, black bile, and yellow bile. Each fluid was associated with two primary qualities: blood was moist and hot, while black bile was dry and cold. For instance, when a patient had a fever, Galen thought he had too much blood, so the accepted therapy was bloodletting, for example by placing leeches on the patient.

Doctors in those days were taught that different organs were influenced by different signs of the zodiac, so they needed to know when the best time would be for a bloodletting. In this curious way physicians were obliged to learn some astrology. This is why the University of Cracow had two professors of astronomy—one was in the medical school. Whether or not Nicolaus used astrology in his treatments, he learned the techniques in Italy.

At the end of his second year in Padua, it was time for Nicolaus to return to Varmia. Although he had not completed the third year required for a doctor of medicine degree, it would not be a good idea for him to go back empty-handed. The Cathedral Chapter would prefer that he have some degree to demonstrate that his six years in Italy had not been wasted. But a degree from Bologna or Padua was expensive. It could cost almost as much as a whole year of study to pay the examiners and to provide the festive banquet expected by his boisterous fellow students. Frugal Nicolaus found a way out. He could go to the University of Ferrara (not far from Bologna) and take the doctoral examination there, where he had no friends needing to be entertained.

On May 31, 1503, Nicolaus Copernicus earned the degree of doctor of canon law from the University of Ferrara. He returned to Varmia before the end of the year. Never again would he leave his homeland in northern Poland.

NICOLAUS COPERNICUS
TURENÆUS BORUSSUS MA-
THEMATICUS.

This woodblock print of Copernicus was created from his self-portrait. The lily of the valley that Copernicus holds is a standard Renaissance symbol for a medical doctor, because the plant was known for its healing properties.

CHAPTER 5

The Breakthrough

In the fall of 1503, Nicolaus Copernicus, age 30, took up his duties as canon of the Cathedral Chapter of Varmia. As one of 16 canons, he would be involved in administering the lands and estates belonging to the diocese. In addition to his regular salary he received income from a small property, and also in that year he was awarded the income from a church school many miles away in Wroclaw. The income from the school meant he was responsible for making sure the teaching was carried out, but a local vicar handled this responsibility. There is no evidence that Copernicus ever visited Wroclaw.

For the next few years, however, Copernicus would not see Frombork very often. Uncle Lucas Watzenrode, who had become the bishop, persuaded the chapter to release his nephew to serve on his personal staff. Eventually the chapter even paid Copernicus a bonus for his services to the bishop. The nephew became the companion, secretary, and personal physician to his uncle. Perhaps Bishop Watzenrode would groom him for higher office; perhaps Copernicus had other ideas. Time would tell.

Copernicus moved to the bishop's palace in Lidzbark, about 40 miles southeast of Frombork. He accompanied his

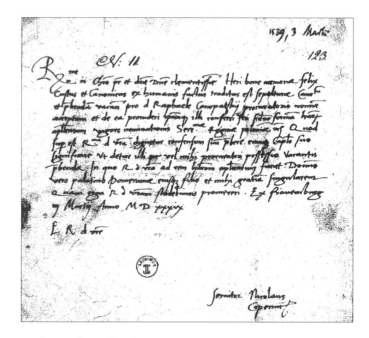

uncle on his official rounds. As the chief administrator of Varmia, Bishop Watzenrode also presided over sessions of the West Prussian Estates, the parliament of the area in northern Poland. Representatives of the towns in the region met from time to time in Malbork or Elblag to decide on matters of trade and defense, and to settle disputes. As chief administrator, the bishop also represented Varmia in pledging his loyalty to the king of Poland and looking after the king's interests, as it was usual at this time for church officials also to represent the monarch. He continued to have to defend his territory against raids by the Teutonic Knights, whose territory encircled most of Varmia. The bishop fell ill in 1507, but recovered soon under Nicolaus's expert medical care.

Despite his diocesan and medical duties, Copernicus managed to find spare time to indulge his scholarly interests. Surprisingly enough, one of these diversions was to learn the Greek language. While in Italy, he had purchased a Greek–Latin dictionary. From the cathedral library in Frombork he borrowed a Greek book that had been published in Venice. It was a large collection of letters written more than a thousand years earlier by a number of Greek authors. To teach himself Greek, Copernicus resolved to translate one set of these letters into Latin. This activity would be essential for him to understand the ancient Greek calendar so that he could determine exactly how many days had passed since Ptolemy had reported various observations. Who knew where that information might be found?

Copernicus chose a set of letters written by an obscure Greek in Constantinople in the late 600s. This man, named Theophylactus, had composed 85 brief letters between senders and recipients he invented based on historical or mythological characters. The main purpose of the letters was to give moral instruction, as with Aesop's *Fables,* the popular collection of ancient Greek fables. Theophylactus wrote his little tales in three styles: as moral advice, as peasant chatter ("rustic"), and as love letters ("amatory"). One set of three gives a taste of what Copernicus was reading:

> **Moral:** You promise much and do little, your tongue being more conspicuous than your deeds. But if you are renowned for the elegance of your diction, the artists wield greater power than your mouth does, since in their paintings they invent such things as Nature cannot produce. . . . Therefore let your actions agree with your rhetoric, lest you be hatefully regarded by your friends as a liar, and furnish your enemies with grounds for assailing you as indifferent to the truth.

The pointed arches of the doors and windows of the bishop's palace at Lidzbark are typical of the early Polish brick gothic style of architecture. Copernicus lived in this palace from 1503 to 1510 while assisting his uncle, Bishop Lucas Watzenrode.

Nearly everyone knows someone who is a big talker, fluent with fancy words, but perhaps weak on action. Clearly this type of character has been around for centuries. But Theophylactus's moral advice is not great literature, whether in Greek, Latin, or English.

> **Rustic:** You wretch, why in the world did you change your clothes and let the partridges fly away. Wine was your trouble. . . . Therefore, unless you recover the birds, together with you I shall jump off a cliff. For a boy to live a bad life is hard to bear. But if a son claims his grave sooner than his father does, that is more unendurable.

This rambling set of advice certainly qualifies as peasant chatter, and why the writer proposes to jump off a cliff rather than just giving the delinquent wretch a shove is hard to fathom.

> **Amorous** [from Thetis to her boyfriend]: You cannot love Thetis and Galatea at the same time. For passions do not engage in struggle, since love is not divided. Nor will you endure a twofold involvement. For just as the earth cannot be warmed by two suns, so one heart does not support two flames of love.

The title page of Copernicus's Latin translation of the "moral, rustic, and amatory letters" of the Greek author Theophylactus Simocatta, printed in 1509. The coats of arms are for Poland, Cracow, and Lithuania, and appeared on many of the books printed in Cracow by Jan Heller, whose initial "h" appears at the bottom center.

Scholars have shown that Copernicus made numerous mistranslations. Nevertheless, he was proud of his effort and showed it to his friends. One of them was so impressed that he wrote an introductory poem and took the manuscript to Cracow, where it was published in 1509. In a short letter to his uncle that prefaced the letters, Coppernicus (for this is how he spelled his name in his first published work) applauded Theophylactus for his compact rules of behavior, and for so mixing "the gay with the serious, and the playful with the austere, that every reader may pluck what pleases him most in these letters, like an assortment of flowers in a garden."

During these years, Copernicus did not entirely neglect astronomy. In 1504, shortly after he had returned from Italy, the planets had bunched up in the sky (a great conjunction) in the constellation of Cancer. Such configurations are uncommon—Jupiter catches up with the slower-moving Saturn only every 20 years. Copernicus watched this stately dance of the planets, carefully comparing their positions with those predicted from astronomical tables. He saw that something was wrong. Although the predicted positions for Jupiter were very accurate, Mars was running ahead of the predictions, and Saturn behind.

At the same time, Copernicus continued to work through Regiomontanus's *Epitome of the Almagest*. The *Epitome* is both a summary and an analysis of Ptolemy's *Almagest*. In some places, Regiomontanus provided clearer explanations than Ptolemy had. And sometimes he went into more detail. The *Epitome* follows the same structure as the *Almagest*; each is composed of 13 books. When Copernicus got to Book 12, he found that Ptolemy had

This rare manuscript in Copernicus's handwriting shows the intermediate stage of the calculations that led to his heliocentric system. Copernicus wrote the note on a blank page in an astronomy book he had bought earlier, while a student in Cracow.

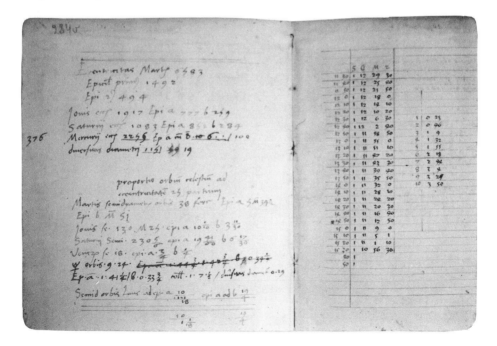

briefly considered an alternative to the epicyclic model for the retrograde motions of the planets. And Regiomontanus had delved into it in even greater detail than Ptolemy. Regiomontanus showed how the role of Ptolemy's large circle (the *deferent,* which carried the epicycle) could be interchanged with the epicycle. This is a very important transformation, because it demonstrated a key step toward finding a sun-centered system.

The figure on this page shows how to interchange the epicycle and the deferent. The heavy line EP is the important sight line from the earth to the planet—in other words, it specifies where to look in the sky for the planet. In order to calculate the direction of the sight line EP, Ptolemy combined the line to the deferent ED, with the line DP for the motion of the planet in the epicycle. (Because trigonometry was not yet well developed in Ptolemy's day, the calculation was pretty tedious.) What Regiomontanus showed was that you could use two identical lines (shown in the diagram as dashed lines) to construct a parallelogram, and that he could calculate the sight line the other way around, using ES and SP. Then the small circle (the former epicycle) goes around the earth and the big circle (the former deferent) pivots around point S. (Interesting, but it does not save any work because the mathematics is just the same.)

But now something almost magical happened. Copernicus noticed that the line ES *always pointed in the direction of the sun.* If he scaled the sun's orbit correctly, the sun would sit at point S, and the planet P would be going around the sun. Copernicus made this interchange for the

Regiomontanus pointed out that there are two equivalent ways to calculate the sight line to a planet, either using the path of the epicycle, EDP, or the alternate ESP.

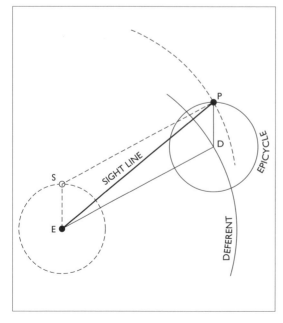

models of Mars, Jupiter, and Saturn, and he placed the sun at the point S in each model. Now the trick was to scale the diagrams so that the line ES was the same size in each model. Then all the models could be stacked together, uniting them into a single system. In Ptolemy's models, every deferent circle had the same radius—say, an arbitrary one hundred units. The result was that the epicycle for Jupiter was smaller than that for Mars, and Saturn's was even smaller. In the interchange, the deferents become huge epicycles, and the epicycles become small deferents. The deferents retain the size differences that the epicycles had before the transformation. At this point, Copernicus could make the first of two startling moves. He chose (for no obvious reason) to make the line ES 25 units long in each model.

On the back of a blank page in his volume of tables (from his student days in Cracow) Copernicus tabulated the results of his calculations to give the line ES (actually the radius of the small circle) in all three models the same length of 25 units. The result was to change the size of the larger circle in each model, to 38 units for Mars, 130 for Jupiter, and 231 for Saturn. He now overlaid the figures for Mars, Jupiter, and Saturn, with the identical earth-sun line (ES) at the same place in each one. This produced a system for the three outer planets. Each would circle the sun at its own distance, while the sun would circle the earth. This was not yet Copernicus's great discovery of a sun-centered system. It is still geocentric—earth-centered—because this arrangement has the sun orbiting the earth.

Often, great discoveries are made step-by-step. If the epicycle sizes for the three planets are divided by 25, the answer is 1.52 for Mars, 5.2 for Jupiter, and 9.24 for Saturn. These are very close to the actual distances from the sun to those planets in *astronomical units,* that is, in units of the distance from the earth to the sun.

Copernicus found that the next step in Book 12 of the *Epitome* gave a similar transformation for the inner planets,

Venus and Mercury. So Venus and Mercury can be added to the system, also going around the sun while the sun goes around the earth. It is hard to make a satisfactory scale drawing, because the orbit for Saturn is about 25 times larger than the orbit for Mercury, but the top figure below shows a partial arrangement schematically. Copernicus was now confronted with a choice and a problem. Should he choose this rather ugly arrangement or the more elegant one below? If he chose this second system with the earth also in orbit about the sun, that would make the earth a planet. And if the earth is in orbit, it has to be moving.

Now, the whole common-sense tradition of philosophy and astronomy from before the time of Aristotle assumed that the earth was at rest in the center of the universe. Well, *almost* the whole tradition. In Italy, Copernicus had read that some ancient Greeks had proposed systems in which the earth moved. But the earth does not *feel* like it is moving. Both Aristotle and Ptolemy had given strong arguments against the earth's motion. Copernicus could not consider making the earth move without having a very good reason for it.

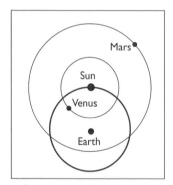

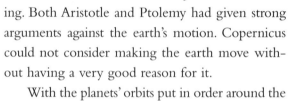

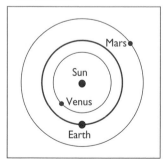

Does the sun orbit the earth as above, or does the earth orbit the sun as below?

With the planets' orbits put in order around the sun, Copernicus realized that this same order applied to their periods (times to complete one orbit). The outermost Saturn took 30 years for one cycle, while innermost Mercury needed only 3 months. The period appropriate to the earth-sun cycle is one year (365 days). As that falls neatly between Mars's period (687 days) and Venus's (225 days), Copernicus put the earth's orbit between these two. He could not put the sun there, because it was already in the center.

Gradually, Copernicus adjusted his thinking to absorb this second startling move. Eventually, he could write in his great treatise, *De revolutionibus orbium coelestium* (On the revolutions of the heavenly spheres), "In no other arrangement do we find such a sure harmonious connection between the size of the orbit and its period."

There was something else, too. Astronomers had never known why the sun was exactly on the opposite side of the sky when Mars, Jupiter, or Saturn was each in the middle of their retrograde motions. In the new arrangement there was a completely logical reason. Mars would appear to move backward when the faster-moving earth bypassed it. And that could happen only when the earth and Mars were in a straight line with the sun.

But there was still work to be done. Just placing the planets in circular orbits centered on the sun would not take care of the details of their motion. Something like eccentric circles and the equant would still be needed. Could Copernicus make it all work without an equant? It was worth trying.

There is no direct evidence about when or where Copernicus's heliocentric—sun-centered—breakthrough took place. But historians, looking at the sparse biographical details of Copernicus's life that remain, the pattern of his astronomical observations, and the fact that a small pamphlet of his heliocentric theory had made its way to a scholar's library in Cracow some time before 1514, conclude that this astronomical work most probably took place in the years 1508–10.

At this time Copernicus made his momentous decision. He would finally choose not to fall in with his uncle's plans for advancement through the power structure of the church. Before the end of 1510, Nicolaus left his service with Bishop Watzenrode and moved to Frombork to take up his duties as canon of the Cathedral Chapter. That might give him more leisure time to pursue astronomical studies when he was not engaged in the business of the cathedral. He was sure he had something, but he could not yet see his way through the haze to a successful resolution of the new arrangement of the cosmos.

Nicolai Copernici

de Hypothesibus motuum coelestium
à se constitutis
commentariolus.

Multitudinem orbium coelestium Maiores nostros
eam maxime ob causam posuisse vides, ut apparentem
in sideribus motum sub regularitate saluarent.
Valde .n. absurdum videbatur coeleste corpus in
absolutiss. rotunditate non semper aequè moueri.
Fieri aut posse aduerterant, ut et compositione
atqz concursu motuum regularium diuersimode
ad aliquem situm moueri quippiam uideretur.
Id qdem Calippus & Eudoxus p concentricos
circulos deducere laborantes non potuerunt.
Et his omnium in motu Sydereo reddere rationem
nō solum eorum quae circa reuolutiones sideriū
uidentur, uerumetiam quod sidera modo scan-
dere in sublime, modo descendere nobis uidentur,
quod concentricitas minime sustinet. Itaqz poti-
or sententia uisa est p eccentricos & epiciclos
id agi, in qua demum maxima pars sapientum
conuenit, attamen quae ab Ptolomeo et plerisqz
alijs passim de his prodita fuerunt, quanqz ad nu-
merum responderent, non paruam quoqz videbant
                                                habere

MS.
HIC.

This 16th-century copy of Copernicus's pamphlet, titled Nicolaus Copernicus, a Sketch [Little Commentary] of His Hypotheses for the Heavenly Motions, *one of only three that have survived from the 1500s, is in the Austrian National Library in Vienna.*

6

An Earth-Shaking Development

Ptolemy's widely-used planetary theories appear to correspond adequately with numerical observations. However, they seem quite doubtful, because they require the use of certain equant circles. As a result the planets do not move uniformly either about their deferent spheres nor about its own center. A theory like this does not seem to me to be complete enough nor sufficiently pleasing to the mind.

When I became aware of these defects, I often pondered whether a more reasonable arrangement of circles could be found. Such an arrangement would explain all the apparent irregularities while keeping everything moving uniformly as required by the principle of perfect motion.

Copernicus, *Little Commentary,* around 1510

On both sides of about six large sheets of paper, Copernicus wrote out a description of his startling new arrangement for planetary motions. The pamphlet did not identify the author and lacked any title. Nowadays, it is usually given the title *Commentariolus* (Little commentary). Copernicus made a few copies and sent them to his mathematical friends in Cracow.

Nothing more was heard of the *Little Commentary* in Copernicus's lifetime. What did appear at the end of his life, more than 30 years later, was something he had promised in that little pamphlet. During those 30 years, when other duties permitted, Copernicus revised and enlarged the work, which was finally published in 1543 with the title *On the Revolutions of the Heavenly Spheres.* Near the beginning of his *Revolutions,* Copernicus boldly introduced the idea that the earth is not fixed in the middle of the universe, but is really a planet in orbit around the sun. For historians, *Revolutions* is a very frustrating account because Copernicus never explains when or why he opted for such a radical, sun-centered cosmology.

When historians discovered two manuscript copies of the *Little Commentary* around 1880, and especially when they realized it was an earlier account of Copernicus's work, there was great excitement because they hoped it would reveal more of how Copernicus arrived at his new ideas. For example, the opening sentences of the *Little Commentary* point out how unsatisfactory Ptolemy's equant appeared in Copernicus's opinion, something that is barely mentioned in the later *Revolutions.*

But this merely adds another mystery. It is possible to find an alternative to the equant, as the Islamic astronomers did during the Middle Ages, but this does not require or even suggest a sun-centered arrangement of the planets. It seems that Copernicus had two separate ideas that appeared "pleasing to the mind," and he worked on them together even though modern scholars have great difficulty in seeing how they can be related. One is eliminating the equant and the other is the heliocentric or sun-centered cosmology. Apparently Copernicus thought both ideas were essential to make a more beautiful view of the heavenly mechanisms.

Copernicus, like most other astronomers of his day, believed that the planets were embedded in transparent shells. Although philosophers of the 16th century engaged in fruitless arguments about whether they were solid or fluid, they had few doubts about their being real.

In the Ptolemaic system, the invisible epicycles that carried the planets were embedded in thick, spherical

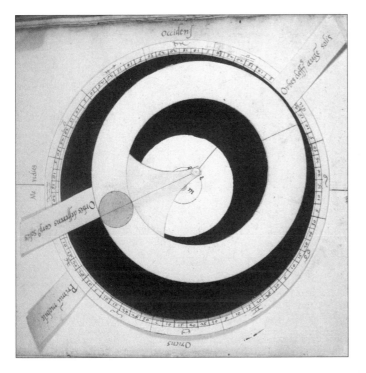

The movable paper parts in this illustration demonstrate Peurbach's model for the sun. The sun wheels around in the eccentrically placed ring, while the black zones fill in the gap so that the similar model for Venus can fit inside the inner circle and the model for Mars can fit outside the large black circle.

celestial shells, as the diagram from Peurbach's *New Theories of the Planets* shows. But the Ptolemaic scheme had the epicycles propelled about an off-center equant point, something not easy to envision in a universe filled with transparent shells. If the equant had its own shell for pushing the epicycle, matters became mechanically confused. In the *Little Commentary,* Copernicus determined to make the scheme mechanically sound by having the shells move uniformly about their exact centers.

The problem of the invisible shells colliding or intersecting with each other became particularly acute when Copernicus tried to merge all the planets into a unified scheme by using Regiomontanus's transformation in his *Epitome of the Almagest.* The figure on the next page shows what happened when he tried to merge Mars, Jupiter, and Saturn into a common system. The unification was wonderful because all the big Ptolemaic epicycles merged into a single circle, that of the sun's orbit around

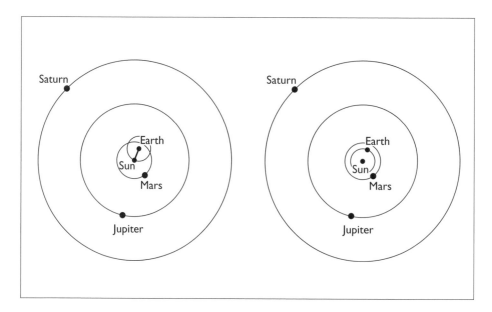

The diagram at the left shows an intermediate stage in Copernicus's thinking, with the sun going around a fixed earth. In this model the moving sun carries the planets in an orbit around it, but there is an ugly intersection of the orbit of Mars with the orbit of the sun. In these diagrams the orbits of Mercury and Venus are too small to plot. The diagram at the right shows the simple, but radical, transformation, where the sun rather than the earth is fixed. The swiftly moving earth becomes one of the planets going around the sun, and the "solar system" is born.

the earth. Unfortunately, the shell for Mars overlapped the shell carrying the sun about the earth. Even though Mars and the sun would never collide, Copernicus claimed that the mechanics of planetary motion would not work if the shells intersected. Actual material shells could not pass through one another. However, Copernicus had a radical solution—instead of keeping the earth at rest, he made the sun stationary in the center, and put the earth onto an appropriate shell.

This, then, is the startling proposal in the *Little Commentary:* One of those planetary shells carried the earth around the sun. Copernicus had followed through his study of Regiomontanus to decide that the planetary spheres all encircle the sun—and that the earth itself is a planet orbiting the sun.

Copernicus had to put the earth into motion in order to avoid having the shells intersect—shells that we now consider to be entirely imaginary. If only Mars had been more than twice as far from the sun as the earth, Copernicus might never have felt the need to move the earth. How different might the history of astronomy have been.

After his brief introduction, Copernicus continued the *Little Commentary* with the statement of seven principles that lay at the foundation of his new view of the universe. He proceeded step-by-step through the items, listing the points where he dissented from Aristotle and Ptolemy. The first three principles shift the center of the universe to the vicinity of the sun, while allowing the moon to orbit around the earth.

1. There is no single center for all the spheres. (Copernicus wished to have the moon's motion centered on the earth, while the other planets' motions were centered on the sun.)

2. The earth is not the center of the universe, but only the center of heaviness and of the moon's sphere.

3. All the spheres encircle the sun, and therefore the center of the universe is near the sun.

A detail of Copernicus's own handwritten diagram of his heliocentric system. Sol, the sun, is fixed in the middle, while the earth with its moon (Telluris cum luna) revolves around the sun in an annual orbit.

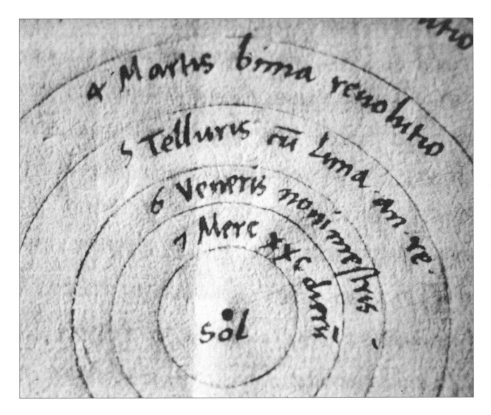

4. The earth-sun distance compared to the height of the vault of heaven (the shell of fixed stars) is so small as to be unnoticeable. As Copernicus exclaims at the end of the cosmological chapter in his *Revolutions,* "So vast, without any question, is the divine handiwork of the Almighty Creator." (This principle is important to account for the annual motion of the earth not being detected by observing the stars; that is, stellar parallax is too tiny to be measured.)

5. Apparent motions in heaven's vault are not real, but result from motions of the earth. The earth rotates on its fixed poles, while the starry vault, the highest heaven, remains motionless. (Here Copernicus gives the earth a daily rotation on its axis to account for the apparent wheeling about of the entire sky every 24 hours.)

6. The apparent motions belonging to the sun are not real but come from the earth and its spherical shell, which revolve about the sun like any other planet. The earth therefore has more than one motion. (Here Copernicus makes explicit the annual motion of the earth, which must be added to its daily rotation.)

7. The retrograde motion that appears in the planets is not real, but is the result of the earth's motion. *Thus, motion of the earth by itself accounts for many apparent irregularities in the heavens.* (This is shown in the diagram for Mars on page 69, where the line of sight from the earth to Mars seems to move backward as the earth overtakes and passes Mars.)

The explanation of the retrograde motion was particularly significant to Copernicus, because he used it as one of his two principal arguments for the heliocentric system in his *Revolutions.* This apparent irregularity emerged as a natural consequence of the earth's motion. He did not need Ptolemy's epicycles. The planets had to retrograde in his system, just as in Ptolemy's, because in every geometric transformation Copernicus had preserved as a constant the

text continues on page 73

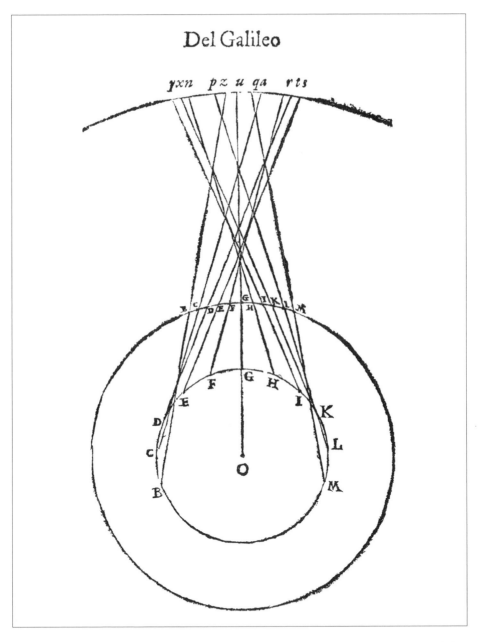

This diagram drawn by Galileo shows how retrograde motion is naturally explained in the heliocentric system. Galileo shows the planets moving clockwise, the faster-moving earth on the inner circle, and the somewhat slower-moving Mars on the middle circle. The lines of sight show how the position of Mars, as viewed from the earth, moves against the background of distant stars, the arc at the top of the diagram. At first from positions B, C, D, and E, Mars appears to move clockwise against the starry background, but as the earth bypasses Mars (sight lines from F, G, and H), Mars appears to reverse its motion against the starry background.

PARALLAX: USING GEOMETRY TO FIND DISTANCE

Both Ptolemy and Copernicus agreed that the heavens are immense compared to the size of the earth. Compared to the sphere of fixed stars, the earth seems a mere point, and the heavens appear the same no matter from where they are viewed. Only one celestial body is an exception. The moon is close enough to the earth that it makes a difference where an observer is located on the earth.

Using lunar eclipses, when the earth's shadow falls on the moon, ancient Greek astronomers found that the moon's distance was 60 times the radius of the earth. As the diagram shows, there is a small difference between the position of the moon with respect to the stars if you observe it when it is straight overhead at the equator and its position when observed at the same time from near the north pole, where the moon appears close to the horizon.

Similarly, observations from a single spot on the earth give a different position for the moon with respect to the stars when it is overhead compared to when it is setting on the horizon the same night. This is because the position

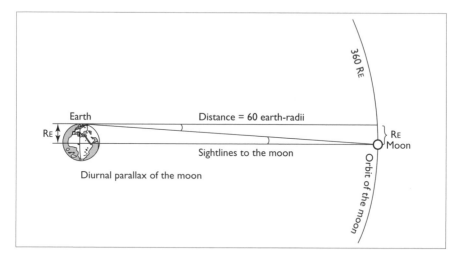

The moon is 60 earth-radii (R_E) distant, and therefore the circumference of the moon's orbit (shown in part by the curved arc at the right) is approximately 360 earth-radii in length. If the moon were enormously far away, the sight lines from the equator and the north pole would be parallel (as shown in the diagram). However, because the moon is relatively close, the sight line from the north pole is slightly depressed. At the moon's orbit this shift equals the radius of the earth, which is 1/360 of the circumference, or 1 degree.

of the observer has changed with the rotation of the earth on its axis. This difference is called the diurnal (or daily) *parallax*. It is tricky to find because the moon changes its position during the several hours between when it is overhead and when it sets. But when the normal movement of the moon is taken into account, there is still a measurable parallax effect. The calculation of how large this apparent change in position is can be easily found in the following way.

Imagine a circle centered on the earth, with a radius (R) of 60 earth-radii (the distance between the earth and moon). The circumference of the circle will be 2 π R = 2 π 60 earth-radii, or about 360 earth-radii (as π is approximately 3). As there are 360 degrees in a circle, a segment of the moon's orbit the size of the earth's radius will subtend an angle of about 1 degree when viewed from the earth. (It may require a few minutes thought to see why this is true.) This is then the difference in the moon's position with respect to the stars when it is on the horizon compared to when it is overhead.

Besides diurnal parallax there is another very similar geometrical tool called *annual parallax,* which works for much larger distances because the baseline is so much larger. Annual parallax uses the huge path of the earth as it goes around the sun as the base of the distance triangle for measuring the distance to a star beyond the solar system.

If the earth is really going around the sun in a yearly motion, there should be some observable effect. We don't easily see it, according to Copernicus, because the distance to the stars is so vast. Today, we realize that Copernicus was quite right. The annual effect on the bright star Sirius is equivalent to measuring the angular size of a dime three miles away! But historically, the lack of a measured parallax was long seen as an obstacle to accepting the heliocentric system.

Not until the end of the 17th century did a few clever investigators begin to appreciate how vast those distances actually are. Assuming that the stars were distant suns, several scientists including Isaac Newton compared the brightness of the star Sirius with the sun, and deduced that Sirius was roughly

continues on page 72

PARALLAX: USING GEOMETRY TO FIND DISTANCE

continued from page 70

25,000 times farther away than the sun, a result actually about 30 times too small! But repeated attempts to measure the parallactic motion of the nearer stars failed; that is, no one could find the tiny apparent motion of the stars caused by the earth going around the sun.

Finally, in 1838, the German astronomer Wilhelm Bessel succeeded in measuring the tiny annual parallax of an inconspicuous star in the constellation Cygnus, a star designated as 61 Cygni. Its distance was 660,000 times farther away than the sun, and the annual change in its position was 1/6,000 of a degree. It then turned out that two other astronomers had also found stellar parallax, but it was Bessel whose careful measurements first convinced the world that the elusive "proof" of the Copernican system had actually been achieved.

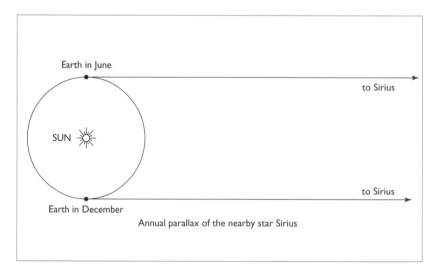

Earth in June

to Sirius

SUN

to Sirius

Earth in December

Annual parallax of the nearby star Sirius

These two lines from the earth to Sirius look parallel, but they will meet at a distance that is 550,000 farther from the earth than the sun. On the scale of this diagram, the lines would have to be six miles long to show when they would meet! The angle between the two lines is ⅙₀₀₀ of a degree. Such tiny angles could not be measured until after 1830.

text continued from page 68

line of sight from the earth to a planet. Nonetheless, it must have pleased him to see that those retrograde motions are not real, but merely result from the fact that we view Mars from a moving platform, spaceship Earth.

Copernicus gave his explanation of the retrograde motion in his discussion of his models for the three outer planets:

> Sometimes a planet is seen to retrograde and sometimes become stationary. This happens because of the motion, not of the planet, but of the earth, as it changes its position on the Great Orb [its annual path around the sun]. For as the earth's speed surpasses the motion of the planet, the line of sight toward the vault of heaven regresses, and the earth more than neutralizes the planet's motion. This regression peaks at the time when the earth is nearest to the planet.

Travel on a modern highway gives a parallel example: when a car overtakes a slower one, the driver in the faster car will see the slower car appear to move backward temporarily *with respect to the distant scenery.* This is precisely the same effect seen from the faster-moving earth as it bypasses Mars every two years or so. Copernicus continues:

> But when the line of sight is moving in the direction opposite to the planet's, and at an equal rate, the planet seems to stand still because the opposite motions neutralize each other. This generally happens when the angle at the earth between the sun and the planet is about 120°. In these outer planets, however, this effect is greater as the orb [or sphere] by which the planet is moved is smaller. Hence in Saturn it is smaller than in Jupiter, and greatest in Mars, according to the ratio of the Great Orb's radius to their radii.

In other words, Copernicus's heliocentric arrangement gave a much more natural and logical explanation of the otherwise puzzling retrograde motion, and, in addition, it explained why the size of the retrogrades differ for Saturn, Jupiter, and Mars.

Copernicus's other main argument for placing all the planets in orbit around the sun was that it put their distances and periods of revolution into a regular order. Copernicus's calculations showed that Mercury in the smallest orbit moves about the sun most swiftly, while distant Saturn is the slowest. And the earth, with its period of one year, has its natural place between Venus and Mars.

	Distance from the sun (astronomical units)	Period of revolution
Mercury	0.39	88 days
Venus	0.72	225 days
Earth	1.00	365 days or 1 year
Mars	1.52	687 days or nearly 2 years
Jupiter	5.2	12 years
Saturn	9.5	30 years

"Only in this way," Copernicus wrote, "do we find a sure harmonious connection between the size of the orbit and the planet's period of revolution."

Were these arguments sufficient to convince the skeptics? Even today innovators often find themselves on a rocky road to acceptance. Five hundred years ago, that road led just about straight up for Copernicus. Almost everybody believed firmly that the earth stood immovable in the center of the universe. They could feel it and see it. Copernicus would have to destroy a tradition that had held all Europe in thrall for more than a thousand years.

He was not at all sure how to do that. Even to convince himself he had to painstakingly create geometrical models for each of the planets (including the earth and the moon). He had to adapt the values for the various dimensions using information in Regiomontanus's *Epitome* and in the *Alfonsine Tables,* the Ptolemaic tables composed in the 13th century that he had owned in a printed version since his student days in Cracow. He had made a brave start in the *Little Commentary.*

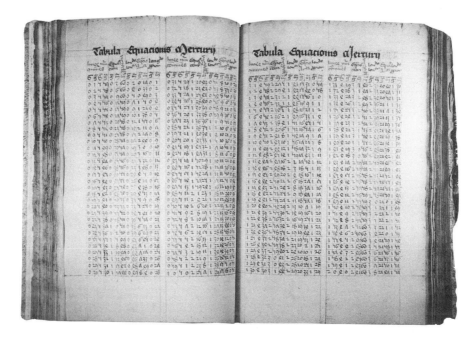

Another successful project had little to do with the earth's motions, but it gave Copernicus confidence. Ptolemy's method for getting the correct angles at which the moon is seen made it appear to change its distance to the earth quite drastically. The moon's distance from the center of the earth is about 60 times the radius of the earth. At certain times of the month, Ptolemy's model put this distance at only about 34 earth radii. If the moon sometimes actually came that much closer, it would appear nearly twice as wide as it normally does. But the moon's apparent size never changes that much (or very much at all). Copernicus improved the model considerably. Perhaps unwittingly, he used one of the revisions made by Muslim astronomers many years before. Whether he learned about their model while in Italy, or invented it independently, we simply do not know.

In 1515, for the first time, the full text of Ptolemy's *Almagest* appeared in print. Perhaps Copernicus was surprised by the differences between the *Epitome of the Almagest* and the complete work. In any event, the appearance of the

The owner of this copy of The Alfonsine Tables, made around 1300, inserted corrections to the calculations for the position of Mercury to adjust for the nonuniform speed of the planet.

printed *Almagest* had a profound influence in shaping his own treatise. He found many tables in the new publication for computing the positions of the sun, moon, and planets. And there was a star catalog with the positions of more than a thousand stars.

Copernicus had largely modeled his *Little Commentary* on Peurbach's much simpler *New Theories of the Planets.* Now Copernicus realized that to make his heliocentric system compete with the ancient Ptolemaic one, he would have to provide a star catalog and tables. It would be a large and complicated book, far grander than the brief description he had recently written. It would need to be a complete revision of Ptolemy's *Almagest,* even replacing Ptolemy's clumsy trigonometry with the more up-to-date version that had been developed by the Islamic mathematicians. This seemed to be the only way to demonstrate that putting the sun in the center and making the earth a planet could provide a way to predict the celestial movements. And for his tables to work in the 1500s, he would have to double-check every number needed for describing all the planetary motions. That would require making fresh observations.

Copernicus had concluded his *Little Commentary* confidently: "Mercury runs on seven circles in all, Venus on five, the earth on three with the moon around it on four, and finally Mars, Jupiter, and Saturn on five each. Thus 34 circles are enough to explain the whole structure of the universe and the entire ballet of the planets." Despite the seeming complexity of the planetary motions, a relatively simple arrangement of circles sufficed for the prediction of the planetary positions. With six planets plus the moon, only seven large circles were required. The remaining 27 circles filled several functions. The earth needed an epicycle for its daily rotation, and another with a long-term cycle of variation in the direction of the earth's axis.

The other five planets and the moon each required an epicycle combined with an epicyclet to replace Ptolemy's equant. In addition, these six each needed an epicyclet pair to account for small variations in the angle of their orbital plane. Mercury's more complex motion needed another epicyclet pair. Using these combination of circles, 34 in all, Copernicus felt confident that he had a model of the planetary motions that could be refined to match observations with great precision.

Making the earth a planet created the "solar system." This system that Copernicus created is coherent in a way that Ptolemy's collection of systems could not be. However, because planetary orbits are not perfectly simple and circular, Copernicus's mathematical analysis required the extra 27 epicycles to make his models fit observations of the planets.

Copernicus had his work cut out for him. For each circle he had to be able to specify the location of its center, the size of its radius, and its speed of rotation—more than a hundred parameters (numerical values) derived from two thousand years' worth of observations. He knew this would be a daunting task. Observing and calculating and checking his models would occupy his spare time for more than 20 years. And being a full-time canon in Varmia and tending to the sick left Dr. Copernicus little spare time.

As a cathedral administrator, Copernicus collected rents from peasants for the farmyards owned by the church.

The Busy Canon

April 1513, Item: Doctor Nicolaus has paid into the treasury of the chapter for 800 bricks and a barrel of chlorinated lime from the cathedral work-yard.

When Copernicus moved to the cathedral in Frombork, he occupied a tower in the northwest corner of the defensive wall. His living and working space comprised three floors of about six hundred square feet each. The top floor had a number of windows and gave access to a balcony. As the balcony did not look out on all sides, he used the bricks and lime that he paid for in April 1513 to have a viewing platform built nearby. On the platform, Copernicus installed his instruments for viewing the heavens.

This was in the century before the telescope was invented, so all his instruments depended on the naked eye. They included a large wooden slab with degree marks like a giant protractor, and an array of big graduated triangular rulers. He describes a set of calibrated rings known as an armillary sphere, but whether he actually had such an instrument is not known. From his viewing platform, Copernicus made observations of eclipses and positions of the sun and planets that would provide the data needed to

establish various values for revising Ptolemy's planetary models.

Although Copernicus must have made hundreds of observations over the next 20 years, records of only about 40 remain. Of these, he would use 27 in his book *Revolutions.* He used them mostly to check whether the constants Ptolemy used to describe the planets were still correct—for example, the relative sizes of epicycles or the direction of a planet's closest approach to the earth. He also reset the clock, so to speak, from where Ptolemy had left it. If the period of a planet's circuit about the sky had a small error, over many centuries the errors could accumulate, just as a clock that runs slightly fast or slow can eventually show a noticeable error. This resetting with observations from the 1500s could improve astronomical tables for a while.

To make his observations and calculations, Copernicus had to find time despite his regular duties as canon of the Varmian chapter. Over a period of 30 years there is no evidence of his shirking those duties. He was a very busy canon.

Within a year of moving to Frombork, Copernicus was elected by his chapter to be its chancellor. In that post, he was responsible for drafting the documents and letters required in the conduct of the chapter's business. He also kept track of the chapter's financial transactions. These were his main duties during the period from 1511 to 1513.

One of the chapter's responsibilities was to maintain law and order in the town of Frombork. In 1514, the chapter renewed the beer license for the tavern, made regulations to protect domestic servants, and sought to enforce the ban on men carrying weapons in the streets at night.

Bishop Lucas Watzenrode died on March 29, 1512. The chapter elected one of its own members to replace him. He was Fabian Luzjañski, who had been a student in Bologna at the same time as Copernicus. The king of Poland (Sigismund I) was not willing to accept this choice without being consulted. For the next few months, the canons negotiated with him over the terms of the appointment of bishops. Finally, in December 1512, they agreed that the king would have the right to make the final selection. The canons of the Cathedral Chapter signed the document, which required that the bishops and canons of Varmia pledge allegiance to the Polish crown. With that, the king accepted Luzjañski as bishop.

Through these years, the Knights of the Teutonic Order continued to sponsor raids from their territory east of Varmia into the lands controlled by the chapter. As these

text continues on page 85

In his *Revolutions* Copernicus mentions three instruments he may have used. We know quite a bit about one of these, called the Ptolemaic rulers, because many years later the Danish astronomer Tycho Brahe sent an observer to Frombork to see what survived from Copernicus's time. His observer brought this instrument back to Denmark. Tycho was very proud of having the Ptolemaic rulers—he immediately wrote a heroic poem to celebrate them—and he described them in his own book on instruments.

The Ptolemaic rulers consisted of three bars, two of them hinged to an upright bar, and arranged so that the shape of the resulting triangle could change. Peepholes were affixed to the upper movable sighting bar so it could be lined up with a star. The lower bar (or ruler) was calibrated for reading the position of the sighting bar. Then, with a trigonometric table, the observer could find the zenith distance of the star or planet—that is, the angular distance from the point directly overhead. Tycho complained that it was difficult to observe the stars through the peepholes, and one could not know if the star was exactly in the center of the peephole when the observation was made. He said the advantage of the instrument was that it could be easily packed up for transport, but that it was hard to keep the wooden rulers from warping.

Copernicus described another, simpler instrument that was a sort of sundial for measuring the altitude of the sun at noon. He said it could be made

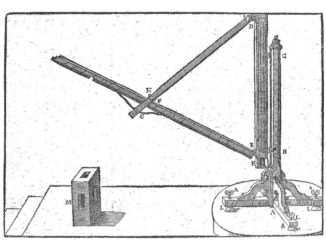

Tycho Brahe's illustration of his Ptolemaic rulers was published in his 1598 book, Instruments for the Reform of Astronomy. *Modeled on the device Copernicus used, Brahe's rulers had several technical improvements.*

from a square of wood, though stone or metal would be better, and he explained how it could be set up accurately in a north–south line. On the square was inscribed a quarter circle marked in degrees, so the instrument is called a quadrant. Because it is a comparatively easy instrument to make, he probably experimented with more than one.

Copernicus is not very explicit about specific observations he made with such a quadrant, though he says he observed the times of the equinoxes for more than 10 years. To determine the day of the equinox, when the sun is midway between its northernmost and southernmost travels (and therefore on the celestial equator), he had to mark the highest and lowest positions of the noon shadows during the year, and bisect the angle between them. When the noon shadow fell on the bisection point, that was the time of the equinox. On the equinox day in March, and again in September, day and night are exactly equal.

The most complicated instrument discussed by Copernicus was called by Ptolemy an astrolabe. But today we refer to it as an armillary sphere, because what we call an astrolabe is an entirely different sort of instrument, a flat set of brass plates representing the stars and horizon for chosen latitudes. Copernicus probably also owned a modern astrolabe, even though he doesn't mention it in the *Revolutions*. Copernicus describes the armillary sphere as consisting of a series of nested rings, one set of which contained sights for setting on the stars or planets. It is a little frustrating that he doesn't tell us the size of his armillary sphere. He just says it can't be too large or it will be hard to handle, nor too small because the rings have to be divided into degrees and minutes ($\frac{1}{60}$ of a degree). If every single minute were inscribed and the marks were $\frac{1}{64}$ of an inch apart, the instrument would have been about 10 feet across, clearly much too big to build and manage. Tycho Brahe's portable armillary sphere was four feet across, and Copernicus's was undoubtedly somewhat smaller—if indeed he owned one, for he never actually claims to have made any of his observations this way.

In fact, a number of the planetary observations he reported involved alignments, such as when he stated that Saturn was in a straight line with the second and third stars in the forehead of Scorpio, or close approaches to stars,

continues on page 84

continued from page 83

such as when he said that Mars was in conjunction with a particularly bright star in Libra. For these types of observations a precise instrument would not have been required to establish a reasonably accurate position. Nevertheless, there is good reason to suppose that at least some of his reported observations were made with an armillary sphere.

The illustration shows one of Tycho Brahe's armillary spheres. The outermost ring of the armillary sphere (BCE) is fixed rigidly along the north–south line with the top of the ring (B) corresponding to the zenith, or overhead point of the sky. The next ring pivots at a point (C) corresponding to the north celestial pole in the sky (near the North Star), and turning this ring represents the daily motion of the heavens. If this second ring has another ring affixed to it at right angles, this third ring represents the celestial equator. The third ring actually consists of two rings: one at right angle (OP) represents the ecliptic path of the sun in the sky (tilted by 23½ degrees to the equator), whereas its partner is pivoted on the ecliptic pole points (I and K) on the second ring. Copernicus describes additional circles inside the ecliptic circle to carry the sighting peepholes, but Tycho cleverly used the ecliptic circle itself for this purpose, sliding the sighting holes around the circle rather than swinging them around on additional circles.

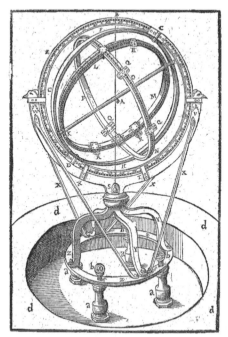

Tycho Brahe's armillary sphere, which he illustrated for his book Instruments for the Reform of Astronomy, *was an improved version of the most complex instrument that Copernicus presumably used.*

text continued from page 81

became more frequent, the chapter appealed to the king of Poland for protection. Matters came to a head in 1516. In desperation the chapter wrote:

> For the past seven years the population of Varmia has endured bloody assaults and acts of robbery directed by the Teutonic Order. As recommended at the last meeting of the Estates of Royal Prussia, the chapter has begun to resist. Two weeks ago, when robbers attacked a citizen of Elblag and cut off his hands, we sent a small detachment into Teutonic Prussia, caught one of the robbers, a nobleman, and retrieved his booty. He was taken into custody along with his horses and weapons. The grand master of the Teutonic Order has demanded their return. Also the robbers have intensified their activities. The chapter begs the king to protect them from their enemies.

The king was sympathetic to this plea, and instructed representatives of the Teutonic Order to stop such raids. They, for their part, denied that the grand master had approved the raids. However, they agreed to raise the matter with him. The king threatened stronger action if things did not improve. They did not.

Meanwhile, Copernicus continued his astronomical work. In 1515, Copernicus received one brief recognition of his work as an astronomer. A Vatican council in session wanted to reform the calendar that had been in use since the time of Julius Caesar. As the year is actually a little shorter than the 365.25 days assumed in the Julian calendar, the time of Easter had been drifting slowly forward toward summer. Pope Leo X sent out a general appeal for help "from all theologians and astronomers of high renown," and an eminent Dutch mathematician, Paul of Middleburg, specifically solicited Copernicus's opinion. Paul listed Copernicus among those who replied, but his reply has been lost, so his opinion is unknown. In his *Revolutions* Copernicus remarked that the matter had been left unresolved because there was not yet sufficient knowledge of the motions of the sun and moon to make a satisfactory change in the calendar. In fact, the change was not made until 1582, when the Vatican arranged to suppress three leap years every four hundred years. That gave the year a length of 365.2425 days (much closer to the actual value). Thus, the year 2000 was a leap year, though 1700, 1800, and 1900 were not.

In 1516, Copernicus took on responsibility for overseeing the properties owned by the chapter in Varmia. This

Varmia, the northernmost diocese in Poland, where Copernicus served as canon, was surrounded by the lands of the Teutonic Knights. This map shows the boundaries as they appeared around 1526.

required him to travel around the territory collecting rents and drawing up leases. He performed these duties for three years, and then again in 1521. Often during these times Copernicus lived in Olsztyn in the Varmian chapter's administrative castle, which was closer to the chapter's main land holdings.

The records of the leases Copernicus drew up provide an insight into peasant life at the time. The land was divided into parcels of about seven acres each. Each lease required a payment of rent as well as of labor for the chapter. The peasants owed their services to the chapter—they were more like slaves than tenants. Indeed, they often ran away to find a better life in town. One large district in Varmia, containing more than 1,600 parcels of land, sometimes had as many as 400 parcels unoccupied.

In May 1517, Copernicus drew up a lease for Jan of Vindica, who was taking over the land of his uncle. It contained four parcels along with "four horses, one colt, six pigs, one leg of pork, one sack of rye, one sack of flour, ½ sack of peas, four sacks of barley, five sacks of oats, one large kettle, one wagon, iron plowshares, one ax, and one scythe." Another lease from May 1521 gives an idea of peasant family circumstances:

> Merten of Lesser Cleberg, father of five sons and holder of 1½ parcels, complained about the small extent of his land. Therefore, with permission he bought 1½ additional parcels from Niclis Ruche. Niclis took possession of two other parcels that were ceded to him by Merten Micher, who is very old and incapacitated, having lost his sons and wife.

Some peasants were in better circumstances than others. And they could negotiate with overseer Copernicus for reduced duties. In 1519 in Voppen, the miller took over 3½ parcels "from which Merten Haneman ran away a year ago." The miller "will be exempt for four years from the annual rent and servitudes, except for hunting." Another man, who already had four parcels in Seefelt, took over 3½

These silver coins were minted under the authority of Sigismund I of Poland in 1535 following the currency reforms that Copernicus proposed.

parcels in Voppen, agreeing that he would "provide someone to cultivate for them"—a budding capitalist! For him, Copernicus wrote: "I granted him exemption from payment and servitudes up to the beginning of 1521."

While Copernicus was overseer of the chapter's properties, he became aware of problems with the value of the coins used in business transactions. A standard coin was supposed to contain the amount of silver that its face value indicated. For example, on that principle, a silver dollar today should contain one dollar worth of silver. Because pure silver is soft, a certain amount of copper was alloyed with the silver to make the coins last longer. Copernicus found that some of the coins were debased—they contained larger proportions of copper and therefore less silver than the standard coins. In particular, the Teutonic Knights were minting debased coins, replacing part of the silver with less-expensive copper. This meant that people who accepted a debased $1 coin at face value might only get 75¢ worth of silver. So, the Knights bought up the good coins, melted them down to produce more debased coins, and made a substantial profit. Those who caught on to what was happening hoarded the good coins, driving them out of circulation.

With enough debased coins in use, they would become the standard. This is a form of inflation: An article that used to cost 50 cents should now be priced at 67 bad cents if the seller is to get the same amount of silver. As a result a good dollar coin would contain $1.33 worth of silver according to the new standard. So silversmiths would try to buy good coins for one dollar and melt them down to recover their silver content. However, because communication was slow, the townsfolk were making money at the expense of the peasants—the peasants did not know they should raise the price of grain if they were being paid with debased coins.

During the summer of 1517 Copernicus took time from his busy activities to compose a brief essay analyzing the principles of coining good money. He explained that "bad money drives out the good money." This principle is now known as Gresham's law, named after a younger contemporary of Copernicus, the English financier Sir Thomas Gresham, even though Copernicus had propounded this idea nearly 30 years before Gresham did. In his essay Copernicus recommended that the king control the minting of coins. At the time, coins were being minted in several Polish cities. Copernicus urged reforms to guarantee that all coins had the value they claimed. In addition, he detailed ways to remove the debased coins from circulation as proper coinage became available.

Copernicus wrote his essay in Latin and gave copies to a few friends. In 1519 some members of the Council of Prussia asked Copernicus for a German version of the essay. He made a translation for them, but the council delayed acting on his suggestions for several years because of an outbreak of war with the Teutonic Knights.

While the Teutonic Knights continued their raids into Varmia, the chapter received no aid from the Polish king. Sensing little opposition, the Knights grew bolder. On the last day of 1519, troops of Grand Master Albrecht of the Teutonic Order occupied Braniewo, the largest town in Varmia, just six miles from Frombork. The bishop sent Copernicus and other canons to negotiate with Albrecht, but he would not budge.

Then, on January 23, 1520, Albrecht's troops attacked Frombork and set it on fire. Only the belated arrival of some Polish troops saved the cathedral from destruction. The homes of all the canons had gone up in flames. The canons fled to other towns—Copernicus and another canon went to Olsztyn. Having endured the Teutonic Knights' steady occupation of more and more of their territory, the canons eventually realized they would have to fight back.

Toward the end of 1520, with five thousand troops in the field, Albrecht was approaching Olsztyn. Copernicus sent a letter to the Polish king asking that the garrison of one hundred men be enlarged. He wrote that the canons depended on the king's care, and "want to act nobly and honestly as faithful subjects of the king, and they are even ready to die." Then, not being sure that he could count on the king for support, Copernicus sent wagons to his fellow canons in Elblag, requesting that they send back food and clothing, as well as a shipment of 20 small cannons to strengthen the defenses of Olsztyn.

Early in 1521, an advance guard of the Teutonic Knights attacked the gates of Olsztyn and killed several Polish soldiers. The town held firm, and just before the end of February the warring parties signed a truce so that life in Varmia gradually returned to normal, though the hard feelings continued.

Copernicus resumed his duties as overseer of the chapter's properties for a short time, but before the end of 1521 he returned to Frombork. In March 1522 he attended the meeting of the Council of Royal Prussia to discuss reforms to the coinage. Members debated the recommendations in Copernicus's essay on money, and decided to follow some of his suggestions. Over the next six years, reforms gradually came into effect: the new standard coins issued by the Polish king Sigismund I matched in value the amount of silver contained in them.

At the end of January 1523, Bishop Luzjañski died. Until a new bishop could be chosen, the canons chose one of their number to take charge of the administration. It is a mark of their high regard for the talents of Canon

Copernicus that they chose him for the post. In April, the canons elected Maurice Ferber to be their new bishop, but he did not officially take up his new duties until October, so in the meantime Copernicus continued as administrator.

In 1525, Poland and the Teutonic Knights reached a final settlement of their disputes. The order of Teutonic Knights was dissolved, and Grand Master Albrecht converted his territory into a secular state, which he ruled under the king of Poland as a hereditary duke. Soon thereafter he

According to legend in 1517 Martin Luther posted his 95 debating theses on the church door in Wittenberg, where he was a monk and teacher at the local university. Most of his theses attacked the lucrative sale of indulgences, papers that supposedly guaranteed the forgiveness of the buyer's sins. His action ignited the Protestant Reformation.

abolished Roman Catholicism in his region and made Lutheranism the state religion. Many knights became Lutherans and married; Albrecht himself married a Danish princess. The few knights who wished to continue the old order moved to Germany.

The religious Reformation, which included the rise of Lutheranism, along with the Renaissance in Italy, marked a move away from the customs of traditional Europe. For centuries Europe's kings and dukes had given allegiance to the pope in Rome and had provided financial support to the Catholic Church. Then, in 1517, Martin Luther, a German monk, challenged the Vatican's fund-raising sales of indulgences, papers that guaranteed the forgiveness of sins. While the church resisted, Luther found support from many dukes in Germany who were jealous of the money being siphoned off to Rome. In a very few years, many of them broke with the church and converted their territories to the new religion that Luther founded. Soon, Catholic Poland was surrounded by Protestants, as Lutherans and other reformers came to be called.

The Reformation had its effects in Varmia. In 1523 the bishop of a nearby diocese published a work favorable to Lutheran ideas. The next year, Copernicus persuaded a fellow canon, Tiedemann Giese, to write a reply. Giese argued for the maintenance of Catholic principles, but used a moderate tone, hoping that the Protestant heretics might rejoin the Roman Church. The other canons (and bishop) of Varmia took a hard line, rejecting moderation. In 1526 they issued an edict banning Lutheran books and expelling Lutherans from their territory. Giese and Copernicus, who favored tolerance, were outvoted.

During the 1530s, Copernicus's active duties in the Varmian chapter lessened. As a senior canon, he became more of a consultant to the administration of the chapter. This gave him more time to devote to the composition of his great astronomical work. However, he continued his medical work when required. In the winter of 1531–32, Bishop Ferber fell seriously ill and sent for Copernicus to attend him. Within a couple of months the bishop was well on the road to recovery. A few years later the bishop suffered a stroke, making it difficult for him to speak. Unfortunately, Copernicus's consultations could do little to help. Two years later, when Bishop Ferber suffered another stroke, Copernicus immediately rushed to Lidzbark to assist, but he was too late; the bishop was already dead.

Choosing a replacement for Bishop Ferber involved the Varmian chapter in considerable political wrangling. The chief contender was Johannes Dantiscus, who was 12 years younger than Copernicus. After years of loyal service to the king of Poland, Dantiscus decided he would like to become bishop of Varmia. As early as 1514, he had tried to get on the first rung by becoming a canon at Frombork. The other canons resisted until 1529, when he finally received the appointment. Then, with the king's support, he advanced the next year to be bishop of the neighboring diocese of Chelmno. Though it was a relatively poor diocese, being its bishop gave Dantiscus a step up on the ecclesiastical ladder. As bishop-elect, he then undertook an extended diplomatic mission to the Low Countries (Belgium and Netherlands). He knew of Copernicus's expertise in astronomy, for he informed one of the leading astronomers there of his countryman's novel ideas.

Once back in Poland, Dantiscus tried to ingratiate himself with the Frombork canons, with little success. However, he did still have the king on his side. As the king backed Dantiscus, the canons elected him to succeed Ferber. Now that the bishop of Chelmno had become bishop of Varmia, his former (and less lucrative) post became vacant. Copernicus's friend and fellow-canon, Tiedemann Giese, was immediately chosen bishop of Chelmno.

With the rebuffs Dantiscus had suffered from the canons of Frombork, he resolved to keep them in line. One of his ways of doing that gave Copernicus considerable grief. Like many of his fellow canons, Copernicus had a woman in his house to cook and clean for him. From time to time, rumors circulated that Copernicus loved her better than was proper. Indeed, one of his fellow canons had fathered children with his own housekeeper. Bishop Dantiscus demanded that the canons give up their house-keepers, whom he accused of being concubines.

There is no evidence that Copernicus was guilty of the charge. His housekeeper was a young woman named Anna Schilling, a distant relative. Although Copernicus denied having improper relations with her, he reluctantly agreed to let her go. There is no record of any illegitimate Copernicus children, although Bishop Dantiscus was known to have an illegitimate daughter. Under the circumstances, perhaps the bishop was unable to imagine that others could behave better than he himself had done.

During all these years, Copernicus continued to make occasional astronomical observations. He knew that Ptolemy's *Almagest* actually contained few specific observations. What mattered was observing the various planets at critical times with respect to the geometry of their orbits. It takes the moon nearly 19 years for its tilted orbit to rotate around the sky, and Saturn requires 30 years to make one complete circuit of the sun. For Copernicus it was more a matter of patience than the process of recording the planets' positions every day or even every month. Whenever geometric conditions were suitable, he recorded positions of the planets, and he took special care to observe eclipses. But he was not a particularly gifted observer, and his observations were erratic in their accuracy. Fundamentally he was a brilliant theorist and careful mathematician, although he also did make enough of his own observations to confirm the essential values he needed for his theory.

After 1529 Copernicus began to compose his book on the revision of Ptolemaic astronomy. While he still took his turn at the various duties of the Cathedral Chapter, he found more time to perform the large number of detailed calculations required. In these he used both observations reported by Ptolemy and a selection of the ones he had made himself. While the manuscript grew fatter, Copernicus made no preparations to have his book published. It would be a complicated book with many tables and diagrams, and there was no suitable printer in the entire region. He was getting older, still a busy senior member of the Cathedral Chapter, but it looked increasingly likely that his masterpiece would simply be destined for a dusty shelf in a sleepy cathedral library.

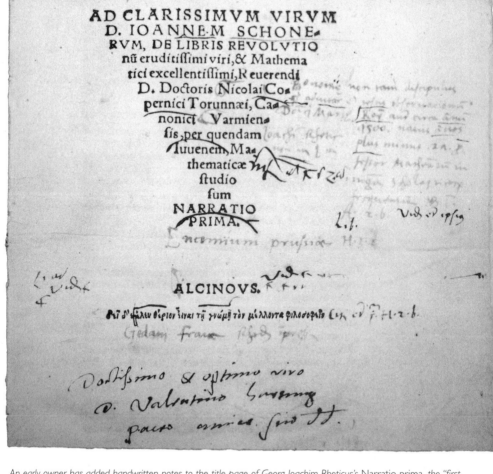

AD CLARISSIMVM VIRVM
D. IOANNEM SCHONE‑
RVM, DE LIBRIS REVOLVTIO
nū eruditiſſimi viri,& Mathema
tici excellentiſſimi, Reuerendi
D. Doctoris Nicolai Co‑
pernici Torunnæi, Ca‑
nonici Varmien‑
ſis, per quendam
Iuuenem, Ma‑
thematicæ
ſtudio
ſum

NARRATIO
PRIMA.

ALCINOVS.

Δεῖ δ' ἐλεύθερον εἶναι τῇ γνώμῃ τὸν μέλλοντα φιλοσοφεῖν

An early owner has added handwritten notes to the title page of Georg Joachim Rheticus's Narratio prima, *the "first report" of Copernicus's new cosmology, published in Gdańsk, Poland, in 1540.*

On the Revolutions

For some years after 1529, Copernicus engaged in the arduous task of putting all his astronomical researches together. He undertook to write a book that would replace Ptolemy's *Almagest*. His book would use his own recent observations to bring Ptolemy's theories into the 1500s. And it would prove that putting the earth into motion was not a foolish daydream. In other ways, Copernicus's book was old-fashioned. It reads almost as if he intended to bring out a new edition of the *Almagest,* "revised and updated."

In 1535 an old schoolmate, Bernard Wapowski, visited Copernicus. As secretary to the king of Poland, Wapowski had learned some details of Copernicus's project. He asked what Copernicus was willing to reveal about his astronomical ideas. Copernicus said he would prepare an almanac of planetary positions derived from his new theory for the next year, but he would not release the theory. That may have been because he was not yet satisfied enough with his book to have it published. Like some later scientists, he might never have been satisfied.

However, other pressures were at work. The general outline of Copernicus's new theory circulated among his friends and fellow canons. In the summer of 1533, one of them described the theory to the secretary of Pope Clement VII. The secretary in turn explained it to the pope and several cardinals. After the pope died in 1534, the secretary began to work for a cardinal, Nicholas Schönberg. After Cardinal Schönberg found out about Copernicus's theory, he was keen to learn more. Near the end of 1536 he wrote a letter to Copernicus. Schönberg congratulated him for having

> fully discussed the whole system of astronomy, and assembled the calculated motions of the wandering stars into tables, to the great admiration of all. Therefore . . . I earnestly and repeatedly beg you to communicate your discovery to enthusiasts and to send me at the first possible opportunity your labors on the sphere of the universe together with the tables.

There is no evidence that Copernicus responded to this request, but he kept the letter.

Canon Tiedemann Giese had been a best friend to Copernicus for many years. He had frequently urged his friend to publish his work—but to no avail. After he became bishop of Chelmno in 1537, Giese continued making arguments to persuade Copernicus to release his great work. Although still unwilling to publish, Copernicus continued to revise and polish his manuscript.

What tipped the balance in favor of publication came from an unexpected quarter. In 1539, Copernicus received a visit from a young Austrian mathematician who was educating himself by consulting scholars at various places in central Europe. Then just 25 years old, Georg Joachim Rheticus had been teaching at the University of Wittenberg. He began his tour in Nuremberg in September 1538, and spent several months there. After three other brief stops, Rheticus arrived in Frombork in May 1539 in order

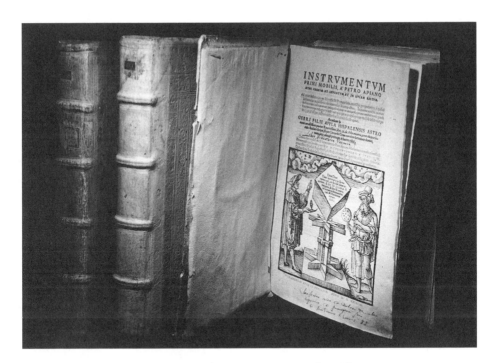

to learn about Copernicus's ideas. He remained with Copernicus for more than two years, becoming the only disciple Copernicus ever had.

Despite the fact that Rheticus was a Lutheran, Copernicus and Bishop Giese welcomed him warmly. By 1539, Protestantism was firmly entrenched in many areas around Catholic Poland: to the west, most of the northern German states; to the north, Scandinavia; and to the east, Duke Albrecht's Prussia—all had rejected allegiance to the Catholic pope. But the recently elected bishop of Varmia, Johannes Dantiscus, was violently anti-Protestant. Despite all that, Giese and Copernicus preserved their tolerant attitude and accepted Rheticus sincerely.

Rheticus was ill for a few weeks during the summer of 1539, and spent the time with Giese and Copernicus at the bishop's palace in Lubawa. Before the end of September, back in Frombork, Rheticus wrote a long letter to a friend in Nuremberg, the astronomer Johannes Schöner. He described Copernicus's work as "six books [parts], imitating

Rheticus brought these three handsomely bound volumes of astronomical and mathematical texts as a gift for Copernicus. Rheticus's inscription to his teacher is visible at the bottom of the title page.

Ptolemy to embrace the whole of astronomy." By then, Rheticus had a general grasp of the first four books, and was proceeding to master the remainder. His letter continued by giving a fine outline of the details of Copernicus's work.

Rheticus also took a copy of his letter to a printer in Gdansk. There, early in 1540, the letter was published with the title *First Report* (*Narratio Prima* in Latin, the language in which Rheticus wrote the letter), but very modestly, without the name of the author spelled out:

TO THE DISTINGUISHED JOHANNES SCHÖNER,
ABOUT THE BOOK OF REVOLUTIONS
by the very learned and excellent
mathematical astronomer, the
Reverend Doctor Nicolaus
Copernicus of Toruń
and Canon of
Varmia by
a young
student of
mathematics,
FIRST REPORT

For the first time, Copernicus's theories based on the earth's motion were announced publicly to the scholarly world. It was a masterful summary of Copernicus's difficult technical work.

Beyond that, the most startling revelation was Rheticus's announcement that Tiedemann Giese had "won from my teacher a promise to permit scholars and posterity to pass judgment on his work." The combined efforts of Giese and Rheticus had at last persuaded the reluctant Copernicus, now 67, to prepare his great work for publication. For the next two years, master and pupil worked on the final revisions—checking calculations, correcting mistakes in the labeling of diagrams, and polishing the language.

Unfortunately, there was no printer nearby who could afford to take on a complicated technical book such as Copernicus's *Revolutions*. It required a printer with international connections and a reputation for publishing scientific texts. Rheticus knew of precisely such a printer in Germany, and in fact he had brought as gifts for his teacher several sample volumes printed by Johannes Petreius in Nuremberg. Rheticus proposed to copy Copernicus's manuscript and to take the copy when he went back to Germany.

In the fall of 1541, Rheticus returned to Wittenberg, carrying Copernicus's precious work with him. He taught at the university during the 1541–42 term. Then in May 1542, Rheticus took the manuscript to Petreius in Nuremberg to be printed. He stayed for a while to check the proofs of the first pages during the printing, but soon he went home to Austria while the many woodblocks were being prepared for printing the numerous diagrams.

Rheticus returned to Nuremberg for some weeks, but meanwhile he had received a very tempting offer to become a professor of mathematics at the University of Leipzig. As a consequence, in the fall of 1542 he left the project, entrusting the proofreading to a Lutheran clergyman in

In this 16th-century woodcut, the printer at the left removes an already printed sheet while his helper inks the type for the next sheet. The frame at the left will be folded down to hold a fresh sheet in place, and it will be folded over the freshly inked type. The paper and type will then be slid under the press, and when the lever is pulled, the screw will be driven down to give a crisp printed impression on the sheet. In the background, typesetters assemble the metal letters for the next pages.

Nuremberg, Andreas Osiander. Osiander was interested in mathematics and astronomy, and a good friend of Petreius.

At the printing shop Copernicus's book was given a longer title. Instead of *De revolutionibus,* the title that Copernicus intended for the work, the printers called the text *De revolutionibus orbium coelestium,* which is commonly translated as *On the Revolutions of the Heavenly Spheres.* When Rheticus found out about the extra words in the title he was displeased, but by then it was too late. The printing of its four hundred large pages took 10 months from June 1542. During these months Copernicus sent to Nuremberg the 1536 letter from Cardinal Schönberg along with a letter of dedication to Pope Paul III—both to be printed in the preface. To the pope, he wrote, "I hesitated for a long time whether to bring my treatise into the light of day," because he was uncertain about how his radical idea of the earth's motions would be received. However, he expressed confidence that his work would be of service to "the ecclesiastical Commonwealth over which your Holiness now holds dominion." And, to forestall criticism from false or unlearned accusers, he sought only the approval of mathematical astronomers who could understand his work: "Mathematics is written for mathematicians."

As the printing of *Revolutions* proceeded, batches of pages were sent to Copernicus for a final check. He sent back a number of corrections to be put on an *errata* (error) sheet that was included with the printed book. However, about December 1542 Copernicus suffered a stroke that paralyzed his right side, making it difficult for him to work. When the printing was completed at the end of March, he had not yet seen the batch of introductory pages for the beginning of the book, including the title page, which Petreius printed last. According to Bishop Giese, Copernicus "saw his work completed only on the day of his death." Copernicus died on May 24, 1543.

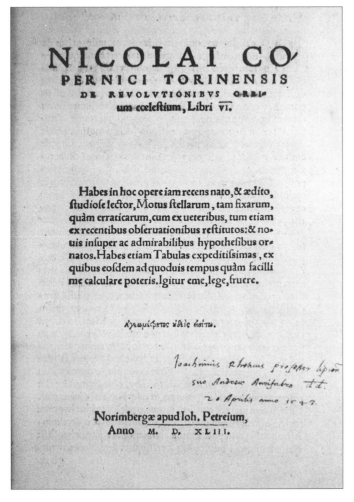

NICOLAI CO

PERNICI TORINENSIS

DE REVOLVTIONIBVS ORBI-
um coeleftium, Libri vi.

Habes in hoc opere iam recens nato, & ædito,
ftudiofe lector, Motus ftellarum, tam fixarum,
quàm erraticarum, cum ex ueteribus, tum etiam
ex recentibus obferuationibus reftitutos: & no-
uis infuper ac admirabilibus hypothefibus or-
natos. Habes etiam Tabulas expeditifsimas, ex
quibus eofdem ad quoduis tempus quàm facili
me calculare poteris. Igitur eme, lege, fruere.

Ἀγεωμέτρητος ἀδεὶς ἐσίτω.

Ioachimus Rheticus professor lip.m
suo Andrea Awifabro t.t.
20 Aprilis anno 1543.

Norimbergæ apud Ioh. Petreium,
Anno M. D. XLIII.

On this title page of
Copernicus's Revolutions,
printed in Nuremberg in
1543, his only disciple,
Rheticus, has written an
inscription to the dean at
the University of
Wittenberg. The partially
crossed-out words
"orbium coelestium,"
meaning "of the heavenly
spheres," were added by
the printer, although
Copernicus preferred the
shorter title.

Many features of the published *Revolutions* are worthy
of note. It is eminently clear that Copernicus used
Ptolemy's *Almagest* as a model for the book's structure. Both
begin with a "philosophical" part in which they argue that
the universe is spherical, and that the earth is very tiny
compared to the extent of the heavens. One major section
of the *Almagest's* part 1 claimed "That the earth is completely devoid of motion." Copernicus titled his equivalent
section, "Why the ancients decided the earth was at rest in
the center of the universe," but immediately followed it by
one arguing that the ancients' arguments were inadequate.

In the longest of his cosmological sections in part 1, Copernicus described the sequence of planetary spheres contained in his system. Then his prose reached a soaring climax as he described his new cosmology. With classical allusions, he made a play for the hearts of philosophers even if they did not understand mathematics:

> In the midst of all dwells the sun. For, what better place could you find for the lamp in this exquisite temple than where it can illuminate everything at the same time? The sun is indeed aptly called by some the lantern of the universe, by others the mind, and by others the ruler. Trismegistus ["thrice-greatest," a mythical Egyptian priest] called it a visible god, Sophocles' Electra, the all-seeing. Thus indeed, as if seated on his royal throne, the sun rules the family of stars circling round him. Nor is the earth cheated of the moon's attendance, but as Aristotle says in *On Animals*, the moon has the closest kinship with the earth. Meanwhile, the earth is fertilized by the sun, and grows verdant each spring.

There is no reason to think that this collection of literary images impressed Copernicus himself. He had derived

This diagram of the heliocentric system appears near the beginning of Revolutions, *where Copernicus praises it as "a most beautiful temple" and "the wisdom of nature."*

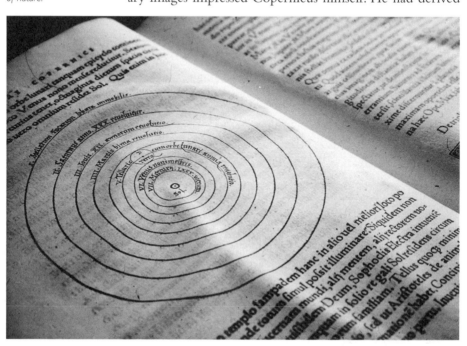

his feelings for the order and harmony of the system from his deep mathematical analysis of the planets' observed positions, not by any means from some mystical worship of the sun. Yet he felt compelled to point out the sun's very special qualities that distinguish it from the planets. Then, at the stirring end of this dramatic defense of his new system comes the zinger—his single best argument for his sun-centered cosmos: "We find in this arrangement the marvelous common measure of the universe, and a sure harmonious linking together of the motions and sizes of the spheres, which can be found in no other way." It was the distance from the earth to the sun that provided the yardstick or "common measure," while this unique arrangement showed how the planets with the longest periods had the largest orbits, a relationship that would later provide the essential foundation for Isaac Newton's mathematical principles of universal gravitation.

Both Ptolemy and Copernicus devoted the rest of part 1 and most of part 2 to the mathematical foundations of their respective systems. They proved some theorems in plane and spherical geometry and described the various spheres and circles needed in astronomy. However, what they included next points to the enormously different views of the cosmos presented by the two astronomers. Copernicus included a star catalog at the end of his part 2, because he considered the outer starry sphere to be solidly fixed, the reference frame against which the motions of the planets would be measured.

Ptolemy's star catalog came much later in his book. For Ptolemy, the starry sphere whirled around the fixed earth every 24 hours, and therefore he next described the sun and moon, whose motions as seen from the fixed earth would establish the framework against which to measure the other celestial motions. Ptolemy realized that there was a subtle difference between the daily whirl of the framework and the spinning of the starry sphere. According to Ptolemy, the starry sphere slowly moved with respect to this framework, a phenomenon known as precession. For Copernicus, this occurred because the axis of the spinning earth slowly changed its direction, just as the axis of a spinning top can change direction. Copernicus's value of 26,000 years for this slow cycle was much more accurate than Ptolemy's 36,000 years.

Both the *Almagest* and *Revolutions* deal with the sun in part 3—Ptolemy presents the "motions of the sun," whereas for Copernicus it is the "*apparent* motions of the sun."

Copernicus described his theory of the moon's motions in part 4. Ptolemy took three parts for that. Here, Copernicus corrected Ptolemy's serious error regarding distances of the moon from earth. Also, using observations more recent than Ptolemy's, he achieved a basis for lunar tables significantly better than those derived from the *Almagest*.

Ptolemy used four parts of the *Almagest* for the longitudinal (east-west) motions of the planets—Mercury in one, then Venus and Mars, Jupiter and Saturn, and one for the retrograde motions. Copernicus considered all these planets in the long part 5 of *Revolutions.* Having led his readers through his cosmological assumptions—that the planets were a unified system, all orbiting around the sun—in the opening chapters of his book, he did not need to take them step-by-step through the transformation from the Ptolemaic epicycles to his sun-centered arrangement. This was a book for mathematicians, so he plunged directly into the heart of the technical details. He showed how his new observations confirmed, or in a few cases adjusted, the numbers used by Ptolemy for the sizes and orientations of the planetary circles. Obtaining these data had cost him many years of patient observations, and had almost prevented him from finishing his great work.

He demonstrated, as he had proposed 30 years earlier in his *Little Commentary,* that he could describe the motions without using a Ptolemaic equant. In the *Little Commentary*

Copernicus had replaced the equant mechanism for each planet with a pair of small circles or epicyclets. Now he did it with an offset orbit and a single epicyclet for each planet, though he carefully described the equivalence of the two arrangements. It was this achievement that made Copernicus, in the eyes of his contemporaries, a second Ptolemy, which for that day was the highest praise for an astronomer.

Both Ptolemy and Copernicus concluded their works with a part devoted to the latitudinal motions of the planets—the way their orbits deviate north or south from the ecliptic, the sun's yearly path through the stars. For Copernicus, that was part 6; for Ptolemy, part 13. This is the weakest and least original part of Copernicus's work. There is even some evidence that he altered it in haste during the time that Rheticus was in Frombork. Did the urgings of Giese and Rheticus force him to publish before he was ready? How different the subsequent history of science might have been if he had never published his *Revolutions.*

Although Copernicus saw on the day he died that the opening pages of his book had at last been printed, he was probably nor aware of their contents. But his friend Giese was scandalized by what he saw. The sheets contained an anonymous introduction that had been slipped in at the printing office in Nuremberg. The introduction included statements that contradicted Copernicus's own opinion about the reality of his heliocentric cosmology, but because it was anonymous many readers would assume, mistakenly, that Copernicus had written it. This introduction, titled "To the reader, on the hypotheses in this book," makes a curious claim. It says that, in effect, the reader should not be shocked by the idea that the earth moves—and should not blame the author for this outrageous notion. He is not claiming it to be necessarily true. The reader may take it simply as a hypothesis because neither an astronomer nor a philosopher can reach any sure conclusion unless it has been divinely revealed to him. Indeed, hypotheses do not even need to be true or even probable: "It is sufficient if they merely produce calculations that agree with the observations."

When Bishop Giese read those words, he was so enraged he wrote a letter to Nuremberg asking the town council to order the deceitful printer to restore the accuracy of his friend's book. Giese also wrote to Rheticus to have the offensive page removed and replaced by a biography of Copernicus. He also asked Rheticus to include a defense of the earth's motion against charges of being contrary to the Bible. However, nothing was done. (Rheticus did write his defense of the Copernican system, showing why the heliocentric system did not disagree with the Bible, but it was not printed until many years later.)

The offending introduction had been written by Osiander while he was supervising the publication of *Revolutions*. This fact was not exposed in print until 1609. Osiander felt that his caution would assist the acceptance of the work, and in fact it did prevent organized resistance from churchmen for many decades. However, Osiander had corresponded with Copernicus a couple of years earlier and knew that the astronomer did not share his attitude. Such differences of opinion about astronomical theories persisted for a long time, and would cause Galileo considerable grief 80 years later.

Many historians mark 1543 as the start of the Scientific Revolution. That would make it the quietest revolution on record. Indeed, the immediate response to Copernicus's *Revolutions* was mild. No serious attacks were mounted against it; nor did it receive any immediate flurry of support. Scholars and libraries across Europe purchased the five hundred printed copies of *Revolutions*. It seems that every astronomer who took his own work seriously wanted a copy. A little more than 20 years later, the book was reprinted in Basel, Switzerland, and spread more widely. During the latter half of the 1500s, the name Copernicus often appeared in astronomical texts and lectures, but usually without any reference at all to the possibility that the earth moved.

The major practical effect of *Revolutions* came in 1551. In that year, Erasmus Reinhold of the University of Wittenberg published a set of tables based on Copernicus's calculations. However, Reinhold did not accept the earth's motion as real. Like Osiander, he considered that the Copernican theorems and elements improved on Ptolemy and were merely a superior way to predict planetary positions. In fact, the accuracy of Reinhold's tables of prediction, like those of Copernicus, were hardly a significant improvement over the *Alfonsine Tables* based on Ptolemy. The reason is that just switching to a heliocentric arrangement does not give an immediate advantage as far as the calculation of planetary positions is concerned. It was just a transformation still largely based on Ptolemy's old and not very precise observations.

And yet Copernicus's *Revolutions* set the stage for future developments in astronomy and physics. Anyone inclined to accept the motion of the earth would have to face its conflict with the physics of Aristotle. Clearly, they could not both be true.

Meanwhile, Copernicus's revolutionary idea lay fallow in several hundred copies of *Revolutions.* The seed began to sprout slowly in the 1580s with the work of Danish observer Tycho Brahe.

The Danish astronomer Tycho Brahe stands heroically with a sextant, an instrument used to measure the angular distance between stars or planets. The book at his feet, On the Recent Phenomena in the Etherial World, showed Tycho's own cosmology, in which the sun carries the planets around a fixed earth, a model that Copernicus had rejected.

Epilogue

Copernicus truly invented the idea of the solar system, the idea that all the planets, including the earth, circle the sun. This revolutionary notion appealed to Copernicus because the whole system seemed so beautiful and coherent. The trouble was that nothing he could say or do made people feel they were living on a moving, spinning planet.

Tycho Brahe, one of the greatest observational astronomers who ever lived, was prominent in Denmark 30 years after Copernicus published his *Revolutions*. Tycho complained that while Copernicus nowhere offended the principles of mathematics, he had thrown the earth into a motion as swift as the stars. For Tycho, the earth was a lazy, sluggish body unfit for motion. Several times he wrote to other astronomers that the Copernican system violated both physics and Holy Scripture. Indeed, Copernicus had been unable to find a satisfactory alternative to Aristotelian physics. It would remain for Galileo and Newton to devise the proper replacement.

In 1596, Johannes Kepler published the first enthusiastic Copernican treatise since *Revolutions* itself. Along with his detailed mathematical explanations, Kepler devoted 10 pages of the hundred in his book to his reasons for favoring Copernicus. When Galileo Galilei in Italy received a copy of Kepler's book, he wrote to him saying that privately he was a Copernican. But at the time Kepler and Galileo were both unusual in accepting the Copernican solar system as a real description of the universe, not just a theoretical model for computing purposes.

During this time Tycho had an observatory where he had compiled the locations of planets and stars for almost 20 years. In 1600, Tycho hired Kepler to help analyze his data. Tycho died near the end of October 1601. Kepler spent five years in laborious calculations and testing of models. While Copernicus had merely put the sun *near* the center of the planetary orbs, Kepler treated the sun as the engine that drove the planets. His later calculations referred planetary orbits to the real physical center of the sun. Eventually, after several years of intense work, he made the breakthrough that makes him famous today— the orbit of Mars is an ellipse, not a circle! Kepler published his results in 1609. His outlook is clearly expressed in the book's title: *New Astronomy, or Celestial Physics Based on Causes.*

The next year Galileo turned his newly perfected telescope to the heavens. Soon he discovered the moons of Jupiter—a miniature solar system in the sky. By the end of 1610 he found that Venus had phases like the moon, demonstrating that Venus went around the sun just as Copernicus had claimed.

Meanwhile, the Bible worried many readers of *Revolutions.* Psalm 104 says that the Lord God had laid the foundation of the earth that it not be moved forever. Did this not contradict the Copernican idea of a moving, whirling earth? In the introduction to his *New Astronomy,* Kepler explained that the Psalm simply expressed God's reliability in making a stable home for mankind. It did not require anything special from astronomy.

In the Book of Joshua (chapter 10), at the battle of Gibeon, Joshua commanded the sun, not the earth, to stand still. But as Galileo advised, the Bible speaks in common language so ordinary people can understand it. Even a Copernican astronomer would use expressions like "sunrise" and "sunset." Galileo argued that "the Bible teaches how to go to heaven, not how the heavens go."

Still, many people were troubled by the apparent conflict between a literal reading of the Bible and the radically unfamiliar ideas in Copernicus's book. As long as astronomers accepted Osiander's introduction to *Revolutions,* there was no problem. He had claimed that the explanations were merely hypotheses that need not be true or even probable. But then Kepler and Galileo began to argue that a heliocentric scheme actually describes nature correctly and that the earth really does orbit the sun each year and whirl around every 24 hours. This offended churchmen in Rome, who decided they had to suppress the idea, fearing it to be dangerous to people's faith. Among other things, they were afraid that the idea of heaven lying just beyond the sphere of fixed stars would be threatened.

In 1616 the Roman Congregation of the Index, an arm of the Catholic Church established to stamp out heresy, issued a decree that said *Revolutions* was prohibited reading for Catholics until it was corrected. Finally, in 1620 (the same year the Pilgrims settled in Plymouth, Massachusetts), 10 corrections were announced. Most of the required changes were designed to make it clear that the heliocentric ideas in the book were simply astronomical hypotheses. One change struck out the sentence where Copernicus exclaimed, "So vast, without any question, is the divine handiwork of the almighty Creator!" Why cancel such a pious statement? Because the Congregation of the Index thought Copernicus made it seem as if God had created the cosmos on a heliocentric blueprint.

This work by John Wilkins, the bishop of Chester, helped popularize the Copernican cosmology for English readers. Wilkins argued that the moon was a world and the earth a planet. Facing Copernicus—who holds a symbol for the heliocentric system—is Galileo, who holds a telescope. Kepler, the first astronomer to publish a heliocentric treatise since Copernicus himself, leans over Galileo's shoulder.

About two-thirds of the copies of Copernicus's book in Italy were censored according to the instructions in the decree, but outside Italy the edict had very little effect. Later Kepler's *Epitome of Copernican Astronomy* and Galileo's *Dialogues on the Two Great World Systems* were also placed on the *Index of Prohibited Books.*

Two generations later Isaac Newton combined insights from Kepler and Galileo to arrive at his own brand-new idea. If left to themselves, the planets would fly off along straight-line paths. They are not "left to themselves" because of a force exerted on them by the sun. And that force is gravity, the very same force that makes apples fall to the ground. Newton published his great *Mathematical Principles of Natural Philosophy* in 1687.

After Newton's work educated people gradually accepted the Copernican system. Eventually the prohibition against *Revolutions* became an embarrassment for the Catholic Church. Matters came to a head in 1820, when a Catholic astronomer wrote a pro-Copernican textbook, and a stubborn censor refused to give the book a license to be printed. Even when the pope ordered the license to be granted, the censor still refused as long as the ban against Copernican books remained. So at last, beginning with the *Index,* published in 1835, the books by Copernicus, Kepler, and Galileo were no longer listed.

Today Copernicus is sometimes referred to as the father of the Scientific Revolution. He toiled away unobtrusively for more than 30 years in a remote corner of Poland. A full-time church business manager and part-time astronomer, he laid a secure foundation for replacing the worldview of Ptolemy and Aristotle—the worldview that had dominated Western thought for 1,500 years. He was the scientist who made the earth a planet.

CHRONOLOGY

1473
February 19: Copernicus born in Toruń, Poland

1483
His father dies; his guardian is uncle Lucas Watzenrode, who becomes bishop of Varmia in 1489

1491
Copernicus enrolls in the University of Cracow

1493
Begins keeping astronomical notes in his newly acquired *Alfonsine Tables,* printed in 1492

1495
Leaves the university without taking a degree

1496
Begins the study of canon law at the University of Bologna; appointed canon of the Cathedral Chapter of Varmia in Frombork, Poland

1497
Lodges with the professor of astronomy in Bologna

1500
Leaves Bologna without taking a degree; spends a few months in Rome

1501
Returns to Frombork; gets permission to study abroad for two more years; enrolls in medicine at University of Padua

1503
Leaves Padua without taking a degree; awarded doctor of canon law degree at Ferrara; becomes personal physician to his uncle, bishop of Varmia, at palace in Lidzbark

1507–10

Around this time begins developing a new planetary theory to improve Ptolemy's astronomy

1509

Publishes a Latin translation of a collection of Greek letters

1510

Completes a manuscript, *Little Commentary,* where he makes the earth a planet orbiting the sun, and sends copies to a few friends; leaves bishop's service and takes up canonical duties in Frombork

1511–13

Elected chancellor of the Cathedral Chapter in Frombork

1515

Obtains the newly published Latin translation of Ptolemy's *Almagest* and begins in earnest to make the observations needed for a major treatise on his new cosmology

1516–21

At Olsztyn oversees the chapter's properties, collecting rents and performing other duties

1517

Composes a treatise on the minting of coins

1520–21

Helps to defend Varmian towns against the forces of the Teutonic Knights

1522

Presents treatise on minting coins to the Congress of the Estates of Royal Prussia

1523

Becomes administrator of Varmia for nine months at Lidzbark

1530

Around this time begins composing his revision of Ptolemy's astronomy, *On the Revolutions of the Heavenly Spheres*

1533

His new heliocentric theory becomes known in Rome

1539–41

Visit by Georg Joachim Rheticus, who becomes his disciple

1540

Publication of Rheticus's *First Report* on the new theory

1542

May: In Nuremberg, Rheticus delivers the manuscript of *Revolutions* to be printed

1543

March: *Revolutions* is published in Nuremberg
May 24: Copernicus dies, seeing his finished work on his deathbed

FURTHER READING

Works by Copernicus

Copernicus, Nicolaus. *On the Revolutions of the Celestial Spheres.* Translated by Charles Glenn Wallis (in 1938). Reprint, Amherst, N.Y.: Prometheus, 1995.

Rosen, Edward. *Three Copernican Treatises.* 3rd ed. revised with a biography of Copernicus. New York: Octagon, 1971.

Works about Copernicus

Gingerich, Owen. *The Book Nobody Read: Chasing the Revolutions of Nicolaus Copernicus.* New York: Walker, 2004.

Kuhn, Thomas. *The Copernican Revolution.* Cambridge, Mass.: Harvard University Press, 1957.

Swerdlow, Noel M., and Otto Neugebauer. *Mathematical Astronomy in Copernicus's* De Revolutionibus. New York: Springer-Verlag, 1984.

Astronomers and Physicists

Christianson, Gale E. *Isaac Newton and the Scientific Revolution.* New York: Oxford University Press, 1996.

Ferguson, Kitty. *Tycho and Kepler.* New York: Walker, 2002.

MacLachlan, James. *Galileo Galilei: First Physicist.* New York: Oxford University Press, 1997.

Voelkel, James. *Johannes Kepler and the New Astronomy.* New York: Oxford University Press, 1999.

History of Astronomy

Crowe, Michael J. *Theories of the World: From Antiquity to the Copernican Revolution.* 2nd ed. Mineola, N.Y.: Dover, 2001.

Evans, James. *The Theory and Practice of Ancient Astronomy.* New York: Oxford University Press, 1998.

Gingerich, Owen. *The Great Copernicus Chase and Other Adventures in Astronomical History.* Cambridge, U.K.: Cambridge University Press, 1992.

Hirshfeld, Alan W. *Parallax: The Race to Measure the Cosmos.* New York: W. H. Freeman, 2001.

Hoskin, Michael. *The Cambridge Concise History of Astronomy.* Cambridge, U.K.: Cambridge University Press, 1999.

Koestler, Arthur. *The Sleepwalkers.* 1959. Reprint, London: Arkana, 1990.

MacLachlan, James. *Children of Prometheus: A History of Science and Technology.* 2nd ed. Toronto: Wall & Emerson, 2002.

North, John. *The Norton History of Astronomy and Cosmology.* New York: W. W. Norton, 1994.

Van Helden, Albert. *Measuring the Universe: Cosmic Dimensions from Aristarchus to Halley.* Chicago: University of Chicago Press, 1985.

Modern Astronomy

Consolmagno, Guy, and Dan M. Davis. *Turn Left at Orion: A Hundred Night Sky Objects to See in a Small Telescope—and How to Find Them.* 3rd ed. Cambridge, U.K.: Cambridge University Press, 2000.

Croswell, Ken. *Magnificent Universe.* New York: Simon & Schuster, 1999.

DeVorkin, David, ed. *Beyond Earth: Mapping the Universe.* Washington, D.C.: National Geographic, 2002.

Dickinson, Terence. *Exploring the Night Sky.* Toronto: Firefly, 1987.

———. *Nightwatch.* 3rd ed. Toronto: Firefly, 1998.

Pasachoff, Jay M. *A Field Guide to the Stars and Planets.* 4th ed. Boston: Houghton Mifflin, 2000.

Rey, H. A. *The Stars: A New Way to See Them.* Boston: Houghton Mifflin, 1976.

Ridpath, Ian, ed. *Norton's Star Atlas and Reference Handbook, Epoch 2000.* New York: Pi Press, 2004.

Sparrow, Giles. *The Universe and How To See It.* Pleasantville, N.Y.: Reader's Digest Books, 2001.

Websites

Ancient Planetary Model Animations
www.csit.fsu.edu/~dduke/models
This site sponsored by Florida State University's School of
Computation Science has excellent animations of planetary
theories from Ptolemy to Copernicus, Tycho, and Kelper.

The Copernican Model
csep10.phys.utk.edu/astr161/lect/retrograde/copernican.html
This site developed as part of an astronomy course at the
University of Tennessee displays the Copernican model of
the sun-centered solar system with a moving graphic to
show retrograde motion.

The Galileo Project
http://galileo.rice.edu
Sponsored by Rice University, the Galileo Project provides
information on the life and works of Galileo Galilei and
other scientists of his time.

Martin Luther
www.luther.de/en/
This site provides information on Martin Luther and his
times.

University of St. Andrews, Scotland
www.history.mcs.st-andrews.ac.uk/history/Mathematicians/
Copernicus.html
This site sponsored by the School of Mathematics and
Statistics of the University of St. Andrews, in Scotland, provides
a brief biography of Copernicus along with many links to
biographies of his associates and successors and features
pictures of many of them, as well as maps and charts.

Wellcome Library: MedHist
www.medhist.ac.uk/index.html
Britain's Wellcome Library sponsor's this searchable catalog of
Internet sites and resources covering the history of medicine
including information on Aristotle and Galen.

ACKNOWLEDGMENTS

We thank Nancy Toff for her patience; it was her vision that brought the Oxford Portraits in Science into being. And we wish especially to thank Brigit Dermott, who carefully untangled a greatly-scribbled-over manuscript with its confusing stack of illustrations, and who managed to sort it all out with good humor and to guide it to a coherent production.

Owen Gingerich is a senior astronomer emeritus at the Smithsonian Astrophysical Observatory and research professor of astronomy and of the history of science at Harvard University. He has served as vice president of the American Philosophical Society and as chairman of the U.S. National Committee of the International Astronomical Union. The author of more than 500 articles and reviews, Professor Gingerich has also written *The Book Nobody Read: Chasing the Revolutions of Nicolaus Copernicus*. The International Astronomical Union's Minor Planet Bureau named Asteroid 2658 "Gingerich" in his honor, and in 2004 the American Astronomical Society awarded him its Education Prize.

James MacLachlan is professor emeritus of history at Ryerson University in Toronto. As a physics teacher he wrote *Matter and Energy: Foundations of Modern Physics*. As a historian of science he wrote *Children of Prometheus: A History of Science and Technology*. For Oxford Portraits in Science he has written *Galileo Galilei: First Physicist* and, with Bruce Collier, *Charles Babbage: And the Engines of Perfection*. He now keeps busy editing technical college textbooks and stage-managing plays for a seniors' drama group.